Arresting God in Kathmandu

Arresting God in Kathmandu

﹏ ﹏ ﹏

Samrat Upadhyay

A MARINER ORIGINAL

Houghton Mifflin Company

Boston · New York

2001

For information about permission to reproduce selections
from this book, write to Permissions, Houghton Mifflin Company,
215 Park Avenue South, New York, New York 10003.

Visit our Web site: www.houghtonmifflinbooks.com.

Library of Congress Cataloging-in-Publication Data
Upadhyay, Samrat.
Arresting God in Kathmandu / Samrat Upadhyay.
p. cm.
ISBN 0-618-04371-3
1. Kathmandu (Nepal)—Fiction. I. Title.
PR9570.N43 U63 2001
823'.92—dc21   00-061328

Printed in the United States of America

Book design by Robert Overholtzer

QUM 10 9 8 7 6 5 4 3 2 1

The epigraph is drawn from Tenzin Wangyal Rinpoche, *Tibetan
Yogas of Dream and Sleep* (Ithaca, N.Y.: Snow Lion Publications, 1998).
Snow Lion Publications can be reached at 607-273-8519 or
tibet@snowlionpub.com.

To Ammi, Buwa, Babita,
and Shahzadi

I want to thank the following people for their generosity of time and spirit, which shaped this book: my editor, Heidi Pitlor; my wife, Babita; and my teachers and friends Paul Lyons, Robbie Shapard, Ian MacMillan, and Mitsy Takahasi.

Upon waking in the morning, think to yourself, "I am awake in a dream." When you enter the kitchen, recognize it as a dream kitchen. Pour dream milk into dream coffee. "It's all a dream," you think to yourself, "this is a dream." Remind yourself of this constantly throughout the day.

—Tenzin Wangyal Rinpoche,
Tibetan Yogas of Dream and Sleep

Contents

Arresting God in Kathmandu

The Good Shopkeeper

Radhika was making the evening meal when Pramod gave her the news. The steam rising off the rotis she was cooking burned his nostrils, so he backed out of the kitchen and into the narrow hallway. When she turned off the gas and joined him, he put his arms behind his back and leaned against the wall.

"What should we do?" she whispered. Their seven-month-old baby was asleep in the next room.

"I don't know," he answered. "Who could have foreseen this?"

"Hare Shiva," she said. "How are we going to pay the next month's rent?" Her eyes filled with tears.

"What's the use of crying now? That's why I never tell you anything. Instead of thinking with a cool mind, you start crying."

"What should I do other than cry? You've worked there for three years, and they let you go, just like that? These people don't have any heart."

"It's not their fault." He tried to sound reasonable. "The company doesn't have enough money."

"So only you should suffer? Why not one of the new accountants? What about Suresh?"

"He knows computers," Pramod said.

"He also knows influential people." She wiped her eyes with the back of her hand, then opened the bedroom door to check on the baby.

"Okay, don't cry. We'll think of something. I'll go and see Shambhu-da tomorrow." Shambhu-da, though only a distant cousin of Radhika's, was very fond of her and referred to her as his favorite sister. He was friends with a number of bureaucrats and had helped several relatives find jobs. Pramod knew Shambhu-da's business was shady; he was involved in building contracts throughout the city that were the source of numerous under-the-table handouts. But if anyone could help him find a job, it would be Shambhu-da. "Something's bound to happen," Pramod told Radhika. "We will find a solution."

Yet despite those spoken assurances, Pramod did not sleep well that night.

The next morning, while it was still dark, he went to the Pashupatinath Temple, made a slow round of the temple complex, and stood in line to get tika from the priest in the main shrine. After putting the paste on his forehead with his third finger, he prayed that Lord Shiva's blessing would help him. When he was young, Pramod loved to visit this famous temple of Lord Shiva, who had protected the inhabitants of the Kathmandu Valley since ancient times. He used to walk through the large complex, making his way among the other worshipers to touch the feet of the gods scattered throughout. But he hadn't been here in months, and he briefly wondered whether he had neglected Shiva. By the time he stepped out of the temple's main gate, the sky was tinged with gray, and he remembered that he would not have to go home to eat and change his clothes for work.

Yesterday afternoon, his director had called him into his office. "Pramod-ji, what can I say? Not everything is in my power." Power, thought Pramod. Of course the director had the power!

On his way from the temple, Pramod saw pilgrims going to pay homage to Lord Shiva. The beggars who slept around the temple complex lined the side of the street, clanking their tin containers. When people threw money and food in their direction, the beggars would eye one another's containers to see who'd got a better deal. The monkeys that roamed the area were also alert, ready to snatch bags and packets from people who looked timid. The smells of deep-fried jilebies, vegetable curry, and hot tea wafted from stalls.

Pramod noticed Homraj slowly walking toward the temple, his cane hanging from his arm. A few years ago Pramod had worked with him in the accounts department of the Education Ministry. Although Pramod turned his face as he passed, Homraj saw him. "Pramod-ji, I didn't know you were such a religious man!" he shouted. Then, coming closer, he added, "What is the matter, Pramod-ji? Is everything all right?"

Pramod hesitated, then told him about the loss of his job.

"Tch, tch," said Homraj, shaking his head. "I'd heard their profits weren't so good, but I didn't imagine they'd let go a diligent worker like you."

The temple bells rang in the background as they stood in the middle of the street. Pramod remembered that he had to catch Shambhu-da before he left for work, so he excused himself.

At Shambhu-da's house, he found two other men waiting in the living room. An old servant told Pramod that Shambhu-da was still doing puja, praying and chanting to the gods, but would join him after half an hour. Pramod sat down on the sofa, and the two men looked at him suspiciously as he gazed at the pictures of religious figures on the wall. He ignored the men and concentrated on the framed picture of Lord Shiva with the snake god, Nag, around his blue neck. After a few minutes, one of the men asked, "Aren't you Prakash-ji?"

Pramod gave him an irritated look and said, "No. My name is Pramod."

"Oh, yes, yes, Pramod-ji. Why did I say Prakash? I know you. You're Shambhu-da's brother-in-law, aren't you?" He was a small, ill-dressed man with a pointed nose and a pinched mouth.

Pramod nodded.

"I met you here a year ago. Don't you remember me?"

Pramod shook his head.

"Kamalkanth; that's my name." The man looked at him expectantly. The other man, who had a broad, dull face, nodded.

"So what brings you here this morning?" Kamalkanth asked.

"Oh, nothing." Pramod wished the man would stop asking questions.

But he didn't. "You work for Better Finance, don't you?"

Pramod was about to say something when the servant appeared with three glasses of tea and announced that Shambhu-da was coming out. Now all three men concentrated on the doorway, where Shambhu-da shortly appeared.

He was wearing only a dhoti, his hairy stomach and his ample breasts bulging above it, and was singing a hymn, one from the puja he performed every morning. After solemnly distributing fruit offerings from the gods to his guests, he asked the servant to bring him juice.

"What brings you here today, brother-in-law?" Shambhu-da asked Pramod.

"Oh, it's been quite a few days, so I just came to see about your health. Radhika sends her regards."

Shambhu-da nodded and turned toward the other men.

Kamalkanth took a sheaf of paper from his briefcase and said, "I have arranged everything here in order, Shambhu-da. All the figures are accurate—I checked them again and again."

"All right," said Shambhu-da. "Why don't you two come back next week? Then we can sit down and talk about your commission."

The two men left, smiling obsequiously, and Shambhu-da turned his attention to Pramod.

"Everything is finished, Shambhu-da," Pramod said. "I'm finished."

Shambhu-da took a sip of juice.

"I've lost my job."

"Why?" Shambhu-da didn't look the least bit perturbed.

"They say the company doesn't have any money."

"Do they have other accountants?"

"Yes, there's a young man who knows computers."

"Ah, yes, computers. They're very fashionable these days, aren't they?" Shambhu-da smiled, then became serious again. "This is no good. No good. Hmmmmm. How is my favorite sister taking all this? How is the baby?" When the baby was born, Shambhu-da had declared that he would be her godfather. Pramod hadn't liked the idea, but Radhika assured him that if something were to happen to them, Shambhu-da would see to it that their baby didn't suffer.

"I'll see what I can do," Shambhu-da said. "We'll come up with a solution. Not to worry." He asked Pramod about the director and jotted down his name. Then he stretched and yawned. The telephone rang and Shambhu-da became engrossed in a conversation, mumbling *hmmm* and *eh* every so often. Pramod looked at all the paintings of the religious figures on the walls—Kali, Ganesh, Vishnu, Shiva—and wondered whether they had anything to do with Shambhu-da's prosperity and quiet confidence. When he realized that the telephone conversation was not going to end soon, he got up to leave, and Shambhu-da, covering the mouthpiece with his palm, said, "I will see what I can do."

Everyone came to know about Pramod, and everywhere he went, friends and relatives gave him sympathetic looks. He was sure that some, those who saw his work at the finance company as lucrative and of high status, were inwardly gloating over his misery. But he tried to act cheerful, telling his friends and relatives these things happen to everyone and that he would certainly find another job. After all, his years of experience as an accountant had to count for something.

He hated his voice when he said this. He hated his smile, which painfully stretched the skin around his mouth; he hated having to explain to everyone why he had lost his job; he hated their commiseration; and he hated Radhika's forlorn look, especially when they were with her relatives, who were more well-off than those on his side.

Every morning before sunrise, he walked to the Pashupatinath Temple. The fresh air cleared his mind, and he found solace in the temple lights before they were switched off at dawn. A couple of times he came across Homraj, who always asked anxiously, "Anything yet?" Eventually Pramod timed his walks so that he would not run into Homraj again.

And every day, after his trip to the temple, Pramod visited people of influence, those who had the power to maneuver him into a job without his undergoing the rigors of an examination or an interview. He tried to maintain faith that something would indeed turn up, that one day he would find himself in an office of his own, seated behind a desk, with a boy to bring him tea every couple of hours. He missed the ritual of going to the office, greeting his colleagues, settling down for the day's work, even though he had been doing the same job for years. He delighted in juggling numbers, calculating percentages, making entries in his neat handwriting. He loved solving math problems in his head, and saw it as a challenge to refrain from using a calculator until the last moment, or only as a means of verification. He loved the midday lull, when everyone in the office ordered snacks and tea, and a feeling of camaraderie came over the workplace: people laughing and eating, talking about mundane things that happened at home, teasing one another, commenting on politics.

Pramod kept up his visits to Shambhu-da's residence, showing his face every week or so, asking whether anything had come up, reminding Shambhu-da of his predicament, playing on the sense of family by mentioning, every so often, that Radhika was his favorite sister. On every visit, Shambhu-da assured Pramod that a job prospect appeared likely and would be certain within a few days. But even though Shambhu-da nodded gravely when Pramod described his strained financial situation, Pramod realized that he had to wait longer and longer to see Shambhu-da. Kamalkanth snickered whenever they happened to be there at the same time. Sometimes when he and his companion looked at Pramod and murmured to each other, Pramod felt like leaving and forgetting about Shambhu-da once and for all.

When two months had passed with no job offer, Pramod's stomach churned. He and Radhika managed to pay both months' rent from their savings, but they had none for the coming month. Although Radhika borrowed some money from her parents, Pramod did not like that at all; it made him appear small. "Don't worry," Radhika said, "we'll pay them back as soon as you get your first salary." She was still trying to be optimistic, he knew, but he no longer shared that attitude.

A few nights later, she brought up the idea of selling their land in the south to finance a shop of their own, perhaps a general store or a stationery outlet. Pramod disliked the idea. "I'm not going to become a shopkeeper at this stage in my life," he said. "I am an accountant, do you understand? I have worked for many big people." Later, while she slept, he regretted having snapped at her. For one thing, he doubted whether the land would fetch much money, because it was getting swampier every year and was far from the major roads. More important, he could never imagine himself as a shopkeeper. How humiliated he would feel if he opened a shop and someone like Homraj came in to buy something. What would he say? Or would he be able to say anything? What if someone like Kamalkanth came in? Could Pramod refuse to sell him goods and tell him never to enter the shop again? If he did, what would happen to the reputation of his shop?

Each night, these thoughts kept Pramod awake for hours. He slunk into bed, faced the wall, and let his imagination run wild. Radhika put the baby to sleep, got into bed beside him, and rested her hand on his back, but he did not turn. Soon she would mutter something, turn off the light, and go to sleep.

Often Pramod imagined himself as a feudal landlord, like one of the men who used to run the farmlands of the country only twenty years earlier. He would have a large royal mustache that curled up at the ends and pointed toward the sky, the kind he could oil and stroke as a sign of power. He saw himself walking through a small village, a servant shielding him from the southern sun with a big black umbrella, while all the villagers greeted him deferentially. He saw himself plump and well cared for. Then he saw himself as an executive officer in a multinational company where Shambhu-da worked as an office boy. Shambhu-da was knocking on the door of Pramod's spacious, air-conditioned office, where he sat behind a large desk in a clean white shirt and tie, his glasses hanging from his neck, a cigarette smoldering on the ashtray. Shambhu-da would walk in, his cheeks hollow, wearing clothes that were clearly second-hand, and plead for an advance on his wages, which Pramod would refuse. Shambhu-da would weep, and Pramod, irritated, would tell him the company had no place for a whiner.

Pramod giggled at this little scene. Then when he realized what he was doing, a moan escaped his lips. Radhika sat up, turned on the light, and asked, "What's the matter? Having a bad dream?"

One morning Pramod was sitting on a bench in the city park, smoking a cigarette, after having made his humiliating morning round, when a small, plump young woman sat next to him and started shelling peanuts that were bundled at the end of her dhoti. The cracking of the shells was getting on his nerves, and he was just about to leave when the woman said, "Do you want some peanuts?"

Pramod shook his head.

"They're very good," she said. "Nicely roasted and salty." She looked like a laborer, or perhaps a village woman working in the city as a servant.

"I don't eat peanuts in the morning," said Pramod.

"Oh, really? I can eat them all day long. Morning, noon, night."

Pramod watched a couple of men in suits and ties, carrying briefcases, enter an office building across the street.

"The mornings here are so beautiful, no?" he heard the woman say. "I come here every day." She popped more peanuts into her mouth. "Where do you work?"

The gall of this woman, clearly of a class much below his. "In an office," he replied.

"It's nearly ten o'clock. Don't you have to go to your office? It's not a holiday today, is it?"

"No, it's not a holiday."

"I just finished my work. Holiday or no holiday, I have to work."

"Where?" asked Pramod.

"In Putalisadak," she said. "I wash clothes, clean the house. But only in the mornings. They have another servant, but she goes to school in the morning. My mistress is very generous."

"Where's your husband?" asked Pramod. He felt himself smile; talking to a servant girl in the park was an indication, he thought, of just how low he had fallen.

"He's back in the village, near Pokhara. He's a carpenter, building this and that. But the money is never enough. That's why I had to come here."

"You don't have any children?"

She shook her head and blushed.

They sat in silence for a moment. She said, "You know, my husband says one shouldn't think too much." There was a note of pity in her voice.

"Why does he say that? Does he say it to you?"

"Not me. I don't think all that much. What's there to think about? Life is what God gives us. My husband says it to any of our relatives who is unhappy and comes to him for advice. In this city I see so many worried people. They walk around not looking at anyone, always thinking, always fretting. This problem, that problem. Sometimes I think if I stay here too long, I'll become like them."

Pramod sighed at her simple ways.

By now the streets were crowded; people were on their way to work. The park, in the center of the city, provided a good view of the surrounding buildings, many of them filled with major offices.

The woman stood, stretched, and said, "Well, I should be going home. Make tea and then cook some rice for myself." She looked at him sweetly. "I can make tea for you in my room."

Pramod was startled.

"It's all right," she said. "You don't have to come if you don't want to. Here you are, sitting and worrying about what, I don't know. So I thought you might want some tea. My house isn't far. It's right here in Asan." She pointed in the direction of the large marketplace.

"All right," Pramod said. He got up and followed her out of the park, embarrassed to be walking beside this servant girl, afraid that someone he knew might see him. But he could feel a slow excitement rising in his body. He walked a few steps behind her, and she, seeming to sense his discomfort, didn't turn around and talk to him.

When they entered Asan, they were swept into the crowd, but he maintained his distance behind her, keeping her red dhoti in sight. There was a pleasant buzz in his ears, as if whatever was happening to him was unreal, as if the events of the last two months were also not true. His worrying was replaced by a lightness. He floated behind her, and the crowd in the marketplace moved forward. He didn't feel constricted, as he usually did in such places. In fact, his heart seemed to have expanded.

When they reached an old house in a narrow alley, she turned around at the doorway and said, "I have a room on the third floor, the other side." She led him through a dirty courtyard, where children were playing marbles, and beckoned to him to follow her through another door. Pramod found himself in the dark. He could hear the swish of her dhoti. "The stairs are here," she said. "Be careful; they're narrow. Watch your head." He reached for her hand, and she held his as she led him up the wooden stairs. Now Pramod could see the faint outline of a door. "One more floor." He thought she looked pretty in that semidarkness. On the next landing she unlocked a door and they entered a small room.

In one corner were a stove and some pots and pans; in another, a cot. A poster of Lord Krishna, his blue chubby face smiling at no one in particular, hung above the bed. The gray light filtering through the small window illuminated the woman's face and objects in the room. She was smiling.

He was drawn to the window, where he was surprised to find a view of the center of the marketplace. He had never before been inside a house in this congested quarter. In the distance, vegetable sellers squatted next to their baskets, smoking and laughing. A faint noise from the market drifted into the room, like the hum of a bee, and he stood at the window and gazed over the rooftops and windows of other houses crammed into this section of the city.

"You can sit on the bed," she said.

He promptly obliged, and she proceeded to boil water for tea. He wondered how she, with her meager income as a housemaid, could afford an apartment in the city's center. Then a curious thought entered his head: could she be a prostitute? Yet he knew she wasn't. As if divining his thought, she said, "The owner of this house is from our village. He knew my father, and he treats me like a daughter. Very kind man. Not many like him these days, you know."

He smiled to himself. Yes, he knew. He said nothing.

When she brought the tea, she sat next to him, and they sipped in silence. Soon he felt drowsy and lay down on the bed. She moved beside him, took his hand, and placed it on her breast. He ran his finger across her plump face. Her eyes were closed. He had no reaction except that there was an inevitability to this, something he'd sensed the moment she began to talk to him in the park.

When he made love to her, it was not with hunger or passion; the act had its own momentum. He was not the one lifting her sari, fumbling with her petticoat, he was not the one doing the penetrating. She required nothing. She just lay beneath him, matching his moves only as the act demanded.

He stayed with her until dusk. They ate, slept, and then he got up to survey the marketplace again. The crowd had swelled; strident voices of women haggling with vendors rose to the window. He felt removed from all of it, a distant observer who had to fulfill no obligations, meet no responsibilities, perform no tasks.

When he got home that evening, he was uncharacteristically talkative. He even played with the baby, cooing to her and swinging her in his arms. Radhika's face brightened, and she asked whether he had good news about a job. He said, "What job? There are no jobs," and her face darkened again.

During the afternoons Pramod still pursued his contacts, hoping something would come along, but the late mornings he reserved for the housemaid. They often met in the park after she'd finished her work and walked to her room in Asan. On Saturdays and holidays he stayed home, sometimes playing with the baby, sometimes listening to the radio.

Once while he and Radhika were preparing for bed, she looked at the baby and said, "We have to think of her future."

Pramod caressed his daughter's face and replied, "I'm sure something will happen," although he had no idea of any prospect.

Putting her hand on his, Radhika said, "I know you're trying. But maybe you should see more people. I went to Shambhu-da yesterday, and he says he'll find you something soon."

"Shambhu-da." Pramod suppressed a groan.

"He's the only one who can help us."

"I don't need his help," said Pramod.

"Don't say that. If you say that, nothing will happen."

Pramod jumped from the bed and said, trembling, "What do you mean, nothing will happen? What's happening now? Is anything happening now?"

One cloudy morning as Pramod and the housemaid left the park and entered the marketplace, he saw Homraj walking toward them, swinging his umbrella.

Before Pramod could hide, Homraj asked, "Oh, Pramod-ji, have you come here to buy vegetables?" He looked at the housemaid curiously. Pramod swallowed and nodded. "Nothing yet, huh?" Homraj asked. "My nephew can't find a job either, but his situation is a little different."

Pramod, conscious of the housemaid by his side, wished she would move on. He put his hands in his pockets and said, "Looks like rain, so I'll have to go," and he walked away, leaving her standing with Homraj.

Later, she caught up with him and asked, "Why were you afraid? What's there to be afraid of?" Pramod, his face grim, kept walking, and when they reached her room, he threw himself on her cot and turned his face away. His chest was so tight that he had to concentrate on breathing. She said nothing more. After setting the water to boil, she came and sat beside him.

Pramod stopped his search for a job and was absent from his house most of the time. One night he even stayed in the housemaid's room, and when he got home in the morning, Radhika was in tears. "Where were you?" She brought her nose close to his face to smell whether he'd been drinking. "What's happened to you? Don't you know that you are a father? A husband?"

Now when he went to family gatherings, he wasn't surprised that the relatives looked at him questioningly. The bold ones even mocked him. "Pramod-ji, a man should not give up so easily. Otherwise he is not a man." Some sought to counsel him. "Radhika is worried about you. These things happen to everyone, but one shouldn't let everything go just like that." He didn't feel he had to respond to them, so he sat in silence, nodding. His father-in-law stopped talking to him, and his mother-in-law's face was strained whenever she had to speak to him.

At a relative's feast one bright afternoon, Pramod watched a game of flush. The men, sitting on the floor in a circle, threw money into the center, and the women hovered around. Shambhu-da was immaculately dressed in a safari suit, and his ruddy face glowed with pleasure as he took carefully folded rupee notes from his pockets. Radhika sat beside Shambhu-da, peering over his cards and making faces.

"Pramod-ji, aren't you going to play?" asked a relative.

Pramod shook his head and smiled.

"Why would Pramod-ji want to play?" said another relative, a bearded man who had been Pramod's childhood friend. "He has better things to do in life." This was followed by a loud guffaw from everyone. Radhika looked at Pramod.

"After all, we're the ones who are fools. Working at a job and then, poof, everything gone in an afternoon of flush." The bearded relative, with a dramatic gesture, tossed some money into the jackpot.

"No job, no worries. Every day is the same," someone else said.

Radhika got up and left the room. Pramod sat with his chin resting on his palms.

Shambhu-da looked at the bearded relative with scorn and asked, "Who are you to talk, eh, Pitamber? A bull without horns can't call himself sharp. What about you, then, who drives a car given to him by his in-laws, and walks around as if he'd earned it?"

At this, some of the men nodded and remarked, "Well said"

and "That's the truth." Pitamber smiled with embarrassment and said, "I was only joking, Shambhu-da. After all, this is a time of festivities."

"You don't joke about such matters," said Shambhu-da with unusual sharpness. "Why should you joke about this, anyway? What about the time you embezzled five lakh rupees from your office? Who rescued you then?"

The room became quiet. Shambhu-da himself looked surprised that he'd mentioned that incident.

Pitamber threw his cards on the floor and stood up. "What did I say, huh? What did I say? I didn't say anything to you. Just because you're older, does that mean you can say anything?" With his right hand, he gesticulated wildly; with his left, he rapidly stroked his beard. His voice grew louder. "What about you? Everyone knows you had that police inspector killed. We aren't fools. How do you make all your money, donkey?"

The use of the word *donkey* prompted the other men to stand and try to restrain Pitamber, who seemed ready to froth at the mouth. "Enough, enough!" cried one woman.

Radhika came back. "What happened?"

A shadow covered Shambhu-da's face, and he too got up. "What do you think, huh? What do you think? Say that again, you motherfucker; just say that again. I can buy people like you with my left hand."

Radhika went over to Pramod and said, "See what you've started?"

Bitterly, he said, "You are a fool," and walked out of the room.

He was engulfed by numbness; things disappeared in a haze. Words and phrases floated through his mind. He remembered stories of people jumping into the Ranipokhari Pond at the center of the city and being sucked under to their death. Could he do it?

Pramod walked the two miles to Asan and moved through the darkness of the staircase to the housemaid's room.

She was pleased to see him.

"I'd like to lie down," he told her.

"Shall I make you tea?"

He shook his head and sank onto her cot. It smelled of her sweat and hair oil. He felt like a patient, ready to be anesthetized so that his body could be torn apart.

"Are you all right?" She put her palm on his forehead.

He nodded and fell asleep. It was a short sleep, filled with jerky images that he forgot when he woke.

She was cooking rice. "You'll eat here?"

For a while, he said nothing. Then he asked, "Aren't you afraid your husband will come? Unannounced?"

She laughed, stirring the rice. "He'd catch us, wouldn't he?"

"What would you do?"

"What would I do?"

"Yes. What would you say to him if he catches us?"

"I don't know," she said. "I never think about it."

"Why?"

"It's not in my nature." She took the rice pot off the stove and put on another, into which she poured clarified butter. She dipped some spinach into the burning ghee; it made a *swoosh*, and smoke rose in a gust. Pramod pulled out a cigarette and set it between his lips without lighting it.

"You know," she said, "if this bothers you, you should go back to your wife."

"It doesn't bother me."

"Sometimes you look worried. As if someone is waiting to catch you."

"Really?" He leaned against the pillow. "Is it my face?"

"Your face, your body." She stirred the spinach and sprinkled it with salt. "What will you do?"

"I'll never find a job," he said, sucking the unlit cigarette. He made an O with his lips and blew imaginary circles of smoke to the ceiling.

"No. I mean if my husband comes."

He waved away the imaginary smoke. "I'll kill him," he said, then laughed.

She also laughed. "My husband is a big man. With big hands."

"I'll give him one karate kick." Pramod got up and kicked his right leg vaguely in her direction. Then he adopted some of the poses he had seen in kung-fu movies. "I will hit Pitamber on the chin like this." He jabbed his fist hard against his palm. "I will kick Shambhu-da in the groin." He lifted his leg high in the air. His legs and arms moved about, jabbing, punching, kicking, thrusting, flailing. He continued until he was tired, then sat down next to her, breathing hard, with an embarrassed smile.

"What good will it do," she said, "to beat up the whole world?"

He raised a finger as if to say: Wait. But when his breathing became normal, he merely smiled, leaned over, and kissed her cheek. "I think I should go now."

"But I made dinner."

"Radhika will be waiting," he said.

It was already twilight when he left. The air had a fresh, tangible quality. He took a deep breath and walked into the marketplace, passing rows of meat shops and sweets vendors.

At the large temple complex of Hanuman Dhoka, he climbed the steps to the three-story temple dedicated to Lord Shiva. A few foreigners milled around, taking pictures. He sat down above the courtyard, which started emptying as the sky grew dark.

When he reached home, Radhika didn't say anything. She

silently placed a plate of rice, dal, and vegetables in front of him, and he ate with gusto, his fingers darting from one dish to another. When he asked for more, she said, "How come you have such an appetite?"

His mouth filled with food, he couldn't respond. After dinner he went to the baby, who stared at him as if he were a stranger. He picked her up by the feet and raised his arms, so that her tiny, bald head was upside down above his face. The baby smiled. Rocking her, Pramod sang a popular song he'd heard on the radio: "The only thing I know how to do is chase after young girls, then put them in a wedding doli and take them home."

When Radhika finished in the kitchen, she stood in the door-way, watching him sing to the baby. Without turning to her, he said, "Maybe we should start a shop. What do you think?"

Radhika looked at him suspiciously, then realized he was seri-ous. Later, when they were in bed and he was about to turn off the light, he said, "Can you imagine me as a shopkeeper? Who would have thought of it?"

"I think you would make a very good shopkeeper," Radhika assured him.

"I will have to grow a mustache."

In the darkness, it occurred to him that perhaps he would be such a good shopkeeper that even if Kamalkanth did come to buy something, Pramod would be polite and say "Please" and "Thank you." He smiled to himself. If Shambhu-da came, Pramod would talk loudly with other customers and pretend Shambhu-da was not there. And if the housemaid came, he would seat her on a stool, and perhaps Radhika would make tea for her.

This last thought appealed to him tremendously.

The Cooking Poet

He was a well-known poet in Nepal. During the rule of the Rana dictators, which lasted for one hundred and eight years, he had been their outspoken critic, lashing out at their cruelty, writing poems comparing the situation of him and his countrymen to that of a caged parrot, whose hunger is not for food but for freedom, whose only desire in the world is to fly away into the woods. The Ranas immediately banned the circulation of the poems and threw the poet in jail. When the revolution finally toppled their regime (it was a classic rebellion, led by the legal king, who had been treated by the Ranas like a eunuch, locked inside the palace and barred from even reading the news), the poet, generally known as Acharya, was regarded as a hero by the people. The king called him into the palace and awarded him several prestigious titles, including one given only to outstanding soldiers on the battlefield, although Acharya had never advocated physical violence. After the elections—as bitter quarrels erupted among the freedom fighters for high-ranking positions in the government, causing a general climate of corruption and ultimately a severe setback in the economy— Acharya was presented with an award given only to the nation's foremost poets.

Acharya was not dazzled by his fame. His quest for truth far outweighed any desire for personal recognition. It amused and surprised him that people made a fuss about his poetry—some critics went so far as to call him "our Shakespeare"—for he loved poetry as an art, not as a means to achieve personal aggrandizement.

Now, at the age of sixty, Acharya lived with his wife and two children (his elder daughter was married and living in another part of the city) in a comfortable house in a quiet part of the city. Royalties from his anthologies and books of poetry, still used in classrooms throughout the country, brought him a decent income, and he spent his time reading, relaxing, and being guest of honor at various functions at schools and colleges. Over the years he had also been a mentor to those whom his friends recommended as serious young writers. Often he judged a poet not only by his writings, but also, after careful observation, by his character, maturity, and humility.

One young man who presented himself to Acharya made an immediate impression by the deep insights expressed in his poems and the masterly way in which they were shaped, with subtle echoes of the classical tradition, infused with a rigorous quality of modernity. After spending some time with the young poet in his study, however, Acharya became offended by his arrogance. The man kept pointing out the impressive manner in which he had employed certain images and his adroit handling of the language. Acharya, convinced that so large an ego is detrimental to the art of poetry, refused to take the young man under his wing, much to the dismay of the colleague who had recommended him. But Acharya was resolute: the poet does not make the poem; the poem makes the poet.

One winter morning, when the city was waking up, a young man, holding a recommendation letter, knocked on Acharya's door. "I hope I'm not intruding, sir," he said nervously, regarding the poet with reverence. "My name is Giri." Acharya invited him to his study and did his best to make him feel welcome. Giri was a short, thin man, with a tuft of black hair hanging over his forehead. His face was delicate, with an aquiline nose that could only belong to a Brahmin, and his eyes were large, with long eyelashes. His face made Acharya think of men who live under the strong influence of their mothers.

After Acharya's wife, Durga, brought in a tray with tea and biscuits, Acharya extended his hand and requested the young man's portfolio.

It contained an epic, running nearly seventy pages, about a young man's passion for his lover (nothing new there), but the poet had taken Lord Bhima, one of the five brothers of the Mahabharata, and turned the strongman into a jealous and passionate lover. In the poem, Lord Bhima was obsessed with Draupadi, the wife who had been bestowed on all five brothers. Lord Bhima's wish to have Draupadi all to himself disrupted the harmony among the brothers, who, in the myth, were known for their loyalty to one another. Giri's control of the verse was so flawless, his characters so believable (despite the ironic twist of the old text), that Acharya found himself transported back to the era of the Mahabharata, with its clanking armor and noble warriors, its beautiful demure women and royal gardens, thundering skies and the gods' frequent interference in men's affairs.

When, after a long time, Acharya lifted his eyes from the final page, Giri was looking up at the large oil painting of the past kings of the country.

"How long have you been a poet?" Acharya asked, clearing his throat.

Giri jumped as if he'd been caught stealing.

"That is my only work, sir," he said. "About half a year."

Surely he is lying, Acharya thought. Such precision of language comes after years of practice, only after the technique becomes second nature to the poet so that his pen can plumb the depths of meaning.

"You must read."

"Occasionally, when I can take time from my college work." Giri had a guilty look.

Acharya noticed the curtains moving softly in the wind. "You have potential."

"Thank you, sir," Giri said.

"We could work together," Acharya said. They would meet every Saturday in his study, and Giri would present his work, which Acharya expected to be substantial.

Giri was obviously overwhelmed, for he kept saying, "Thank you, sir. You're so kind, sir."

After escorting Giri to the main entrance, Acharya went to his study and read the entire work again, this time with a critical eye. But the poem was almost flawless. For a brief moment, he was anxious. What could he teach this gifted man?

At the academy, Acharya could not stop talking about Giri's epic, surprising his colleagues, who had rarely heard him speak such praise.

"He is a genius," Acharya said in the canteen over a cup of lemon tea. He was startled by his own assertion.

"Then we should publish him," said one of the men who supervised the printing press in the basement.

"No, no, no." Acharya shook his head. "He needs time. One more year." He looked around the table and saw his colleagues nodding solemnly, although Acharya knew they were more interested in promoting themselves than some young novice who had taken a fancy to poetry. Later, the conversation changed to politics, but Acharya found himself thinking of Giri's poem, and he started humming an old song to himself, distractedly, like a man so overwhelmed by a new discovery that he cannot concentrate on anything else.

When Giri arrived the next Saturday, Acharya was playing with one of his grandchildren on the lawn, while his elder daughter, visiting for the weekend, watered the flowers. Durga sat in a white plastic chair, knitting. His son — who was about Giri's age and was studying engineering — and the younger daughter had gone to the temple. The winter sun warmed Acharya's back.

"Come in, come in," Acharya shouted when he saw Giri standing hesitantly at the gate, as if afraid to break into this family scene. "Make yourself comfortable; don't be shy," Acharya said. "Consider yourself family." He had never before offered such hospitality to a pupil, and he detected a note of awkwardness in his voice.

After the formalities were over and Acharya had read Giri's new poems, he once again found himself transported — flying, weightless, over the crowded streets and alleys that these poems described. When he finished reading, Acharya could feel himself smiling. "This is good," he said, trying to calm his excitement.

"Thank you, sir." Giri looked at him anxiously, waiting for the real criticism.

"You could polish your imagery," Acharya suggested, and launched into a long discussion of the poems. Every time he pointed out a small flaw or an area that could be improved, he became unsure of himself. These were minor criticisms, and he was not confident that any changes would necessarily improve the poems. In fact, the minor faults seemed to add dimension rather than lessen it.

After Giri left, Acharya, tired, stared at his empty chair. His daughter came to his side and said, "Is something wrong, Papa? You don't look well."

Acharya shook his head. "Such talent . . . so young."

That night, sitting at his desk and reading a colleague's poems, he was suddenly inspired to write an epic. A major undertaking, but a worthwhile one. As a young poet he had written a book-length poem that he considered a failure, though it was still studied in higher-level classrooms. Now seemed an appropriate moment to undertake another such venture; he had experience—both in poetry and in life. Moreover, he was not oblivious of his advancing age. The previous year he had suffered heart palpitations; lately, he had experienced back pains, to the concern of his family and friends. One colleague had given him a special chair, which sat, unused, in a corner of his study. Yes, this would be the right moment for an epic, perhaps the last major work he would write.

Acharya, excited at the prospect, could no longer concentrate on the poems before him. Resolved to begin his epic the next night, he turned off the light in his study and went to bed. But he didn't fall asleep for a long time; he lay there listening to frogs croak outside and thought about his epic. He tried to come up with a central image that would define the poem, but he was distracted by Durga's faint snoring.

Then, at some point during the night, Acharya awoke from uneasy dreams with a nagging pain in his back. He decided not to wake Durga. His throat was parched, but even after finishing the water in the jug by the bed, he was thirsty, and he went to the kitchen. He could feel the cold water he drank reach his stomach. As he headed back to the bedroom, almost as an afterthought he went to his study, switched on the lamp, and took the copy of Giri's epic from the shelf. He read it again, slowly, noting the juxtaposition of certain words, discovering with each breath the subtle rhyme patterns.

He had no idea how long he'd been standing by the lamp when he saw Durga in the doorway, her stout body like a ghost in the gray light.

"A good poet, is he?" she asked, looking at him curiously, her eyes puffed from sleep.

"Hmmm," said Acharya, somewhat embarrassed.

"The world is changing," Durga said. "A good night's sleep should clear your mind."

Not receiving any response, she went back to bed, and, after a short while, Acharya followed her.

Giri's visits to the house became more frequent. Sometimes he appeared soon after dawn, carrying fresh tomatoes, cauliflower, or radishes in a bag. Every time he came, he stood at the door uncertainly, as if he were not sure of his status with the family since his last visit. Durga became fonder of him with each visit. "Any mother would be proud to have such a son," she often said to her husband, who, although pleased to see Giri, was not comfortable with such rapid family intimacy.

Giri often spent time in the kitchen, helping Durga cook the afternoon or evening meal, tasting the egg curry or fried okra, suggesting new recipes. Acharya's son, the one studying engineering, started to call him the Cooking Poet. "Is this how you cook your poetry, Giri? Fry everything in clarified butter, a little coriander here, a little basil there?" Giri's face turned crimson at the teasing, and he barely lifted his gaze from the onions he was chopping or the squash he was stirring. It was as if a new child had entered the house. Acharya suspected that his daughter, who was barely eighteen, was developing a crush on Giri, for in his presence her normal haughty, impatient ways disappeared, and she acted demure.

Through conversations he overheard and tidbits he gathered from Durga (he never questioned the young poet directly about himself), Acharya pieced together, like a jigsaw puzzle, Giri's life outside his poetry. His father had died at an early age, and Giri had been raised by his mother (here Acharya congratulated himself on his earlier intuition) in a village outside the city. He had a younger sister, who was mentally retarded and lived with the mother. And he had a scholarship that paid for his college expenses and kept him from starving—"such a hard life for a young boy," Durga declared. And he was a member of the United Democratic Front, the growing ultra-left group that demanded changes in the country's power structure. This last bit of information came as a surprise to Acharya, who perceived Giri's radical politics as incongruent with his personality. The few members of the UDF he had met or seen in colleges had a brazen attitude hinting at mania. He had been unable to comprehend them. Yet here was Giri, who cringed before a raised eyebrow.

Occasionally Giri missed his scheduled weekly appointment and then turned up the following Saturday with the bag of vegetables, again looking uncertain. Acharya would scold him for not keeping the appointment, and Giri would apologize and say that he had had to arrange for a "meeting." Acharya would shake his head, thinking, Your commitment should be art, not politics. But once he'd read Giri's new poems, he would feel foolish, because they were as good as ever.

Acharya arranged for Giri to present a reading at the academy. "Just wait," he told his colleagues. "This one is of a different breed." On the day of the reading, Acharya and Giri sat in the back of the car for a last-minute consultation, while Acharya's son drove and Durga and their daughter sat squeezed together in the front. Giri had oiled and neatly combed his hair, which made him seem even younger. He looks like a child, Acharya thought as the car pulled into the academy compound.

Before the reading started, Acharya restlessly roamed about the auditorium, checking to see whether the microphone was working, greeting a colleague he hadn't seen for some time, reprimanding his daughter for her breathless questions about Giri. When Giri walked to the podium, Acharya went to the back of the sloped auditorium so that he had to look down at the stage. The members of the academy were seated at the front, but he did not wish to sit among them lest their faces distract him. After the introduction, Giri, his soft face white under the bright lights, thanked Acharya, without whose guidance "I would not be privileged to stand humbly before you today." Then he began to read, hesitantly. The faint tremor in his voice reminded Acharya of the first reading he himself had given on the same stage, although the auditorium was nowhere as large as it was today.

By the third poem, the auditorium was filled with silence. Giri read with more enthusiasm, occasionally lifting his hand in an awkward gesture or raising his eyes from the pages to see the audience in the darkened room. Acharya noted the attentive faces of the people around him. Rarely had he felt such pride; at the same time, a restlessness swept over him. He could not concentrate on Giri's words, though the poet's small frame on the brightly lit stage was intensely clear, even from a distance; it was as if Acharya were looking through a telescope. He felt that Giri needed protection, although from what, he did not know.

His reverie was broken by the applause that followed the end of the reading. Giri walked all the way up the aisle to touch Acharya's feet in homage. Acharya pulled him up and embraced him. His colleagues came over and congratulated him on his "new discovery" and patted Giri on the back. Amid all the congratulations, Acharya suddenly wanted to leave.

Often when Acharya sat down to write, he was beset by anxiety. His epic was not going well; that was certain. And he started to doubt the quality of his past work. He went through most of his poems and found them lacking. Even the one about the parrot, which had propelled him to fame, now seemed simplistic and self-conscious. Giri's epic loomed above him as the ideal.

Acharya's study became littered with writings violently crossed out, much to the chagrin of Durga, who, after she first saw the discarded papers, said, "Perhaps we should go on a pilgrimage, no?" Acharya impatiently waved her off, annoyed by the thought that religion would solve his writing problems. The more lines he crossed out, the more urgent was his compulsion to write. His back troubled him more frequently—a searing pain extended to his neck—and he found himself using that special chair in the corner.

During his renewed consultations with Giri, Acharya found more faults with the young man's poems. "Here, here, how can you do this?" he once shouted shrilly, and saw Giri's startled expression. Acharya regretted his outburst; after all, Giri was a novice and had to be treated gently. Giri averted his eyes and said, "Sorry, sir, sorry."

Sometimes Acharya despised Giri for accepting the humiliation and wished he were not so sensitive to criticism. A man does not become a poet in a day, he repeated, sometimes to himself, sometimes to Durga, who looked so worried that he became irritable. Once when he confided to a friend, "I cannot write anymore," he felt weak, and the friend suggested he take a vacation in India—perhaps a pilgrimage.

Frost covered the city as winter reached its peak. For three weeks, Giri did not show up for his appointment, and Acharya grew worried. He sent his son to Giri's home, but the son reported that Giri had left the city to join a rally in another part of the country. Acharya felt slighted.

The news of the shooting and the subsequent announcement of the names of those who died came one afternoon when Acharya's family was gathered on the lawn, enjoying the warmth of the winter sun. The radio buzzed on the windowsill and they heard the name: Giri Kumar Rizal. Acharya's son ran to the radio and turned up the volume. Shooting had broken out at a protest march in Bhairaba, and among the bodies was that of Giri Kumar Rizal. Durga let out a muffled scream, which seemed to get stuck in the air as the voice on the radio listed more names. Acharya's daughter put her hand to her mouth and ran inside, slamming the door behind her. His son stared at the radio even though the government broadcaster had moved on to other news. Acharya sat down on his chair with a thump, but he was not thinking of Giri. He was thinking of one of Giri's powerful verses.

The complete account of the shooting came to Acharya in pieces, as did the story of Giri's life outside his poems, from men who had been at the rally and others who had secondhand information. The protest had turned into a fistfight between the United Democratic Front and the rival party. Giri, trying to break up the fight, had appealed for a united protest against the government at the very moment that someone had fired a pistol blindly into the crowd. Later, the police found the bullet lodged in Giri's throat. Meanwhile, in the pandemonium, police had begun shooting at the crowd.

Death hung in the corners of Acharya's house for several days, especially in the kitchen, where Durga said she felt Giri's presence. The daughter was hit the hardest; for a number of days, she didn't eat properly, and her eyes would fill with tears whenever Giri was mentioned. But after a while things returned to normal. Durga once more referred to Giri by the name her son had given him, the Cooking Poet—"Poor Cooking Poet, my kitchen feels empty without him"—and soon they recalled him only occasionally, mostly when they were cooking in the kitchen. Once Acharya's daughter said solemnly, "I loved his poems," although she had never read them.

For a few weeks Acharya was wrapped in confusion; he did not know how to adjust to Giri's death. It was like waking up from a long afternoon nap and finding that you had been robbed. Colleagues consoled him, for they knew he mourned for his most prized pupil.

Acharya thought of the shy man who turned red when admonished and repeated, "Sorry, sir, so sorry." He regretted having been critical of Giri's work. Had his poems really become less effective, or had Acharya's disapproval of Giri's political involvement distorted his appreciation of Giri's work? After all, Giri had lived a dual life, and his political self had prevented Acharya from understanding Giri's true nature. The more Acharya thought about this, the more he remembered his own youth: the protest marches he'd participated in, the madness that overtook the crowd when it demanded the return of the proper heir to the crown, the days he'd spent in jail with common criminals, creating lines of poetry in his mind and committing them to memory. Acharya, looking at himself in a mirror, could not connect those memories of the young poet with the reflection in front of him, the body slouching from back pain, doubt creeping into the lines of his face.

When winter gave way to spring and leaves started sprouting on the branches, Acharya, in fits and starts, went back to work on his epic. Giri's file still lay on his shelf, gathering dust. It had acquired a certain aura, like that of classical texts one treasured but hesitated to open lest they let out some old ghost. Now when Acharya thought of Giri, the image he summoned up was one he had, in fact, never seen: Giri appealing to the two fighting factions, a hand from the side raised in air, holding a gun, and Giri's throat split open by the bullet, blood gushing forth and splattering the men around him.

The words to the epic did not come. Acharya played with language, plot, all the techniques he had learned over the years. During these three months he often stayed up late into the night, forgetting to eat, and his body looked frail as dark circles appeared around his eyes. Twice he had to be rushed to the hospital with excruciating back pain.

One night, after he had torn to shreds nearly twenty of his recent verses, Acharya lay his head on the desk and abandoned the task. All the versions had been mediocre at best; he needed no one to tell him this. Nor did he have any intention of revealing his work, for he did not wish to display the degeneration of his art, which had brought pleasure to men for years. Quietly, but resolutely, he shut his notebook and left the study.

When the government announced that Acharya was to be named the poet laureate of the country, his family members and friends could barely contain their joy. The Poetry Committee of the academy, with the active endorsement of the king, decided that, in commemoration of the twenty-fifth anniversary of the revolution, Acharya should be honored not only for his participation in the revolution but also for his commitment to poetry and art, as substantiated by his prodigious body of work. "We were not wrong," wrote one of the critics who had earlier called him "our Shakespeare." "Acharya has proven himself the equal of any acclaimed author today," and he went on to list some of the giants in poetry, such as Pablo Neruda, Czeslaw Milosz, and Faiz Ahmed Faiz. Posters of Acharya from his earlier days appeared all over the country. He received letters of congratulations from famous poets in neighboring countries, and a procession was organized to take place after the awards ceremony.

The academy auditorium was filled with dignitaries and high government officials. A red banner with Acharya's name hung at the back of the stage. Well-known poets praised Acharya's poetry and his contribution to Nepali literature. Acharya, sitting in the front with the country's prime minister, who would soon present the award, watched the ceremony in a daze, the noise buzzing around him.

The prime minister gave a short speech, and Acharya made his way to the stage to receive the gold trophy, a small statue of a famous seventeenth-century poet. He thanked his family and friends for their support.

After a few words, he was about to head back to his seat when he glanced at the silver lights focused on the middle of the stage and remembered Giri reading in that auditorium, his white face shining in the darkness. Acharya felt paralyzed, as if stricken by stage fright. He did not see any faces, only dim figures that could be sitting, standing, dancing in the dark, offering applause that rose and fell, rose and fell, until a steady din started circling the high walls and ceiling of the auditorium.

Deepak Misra's Secretary

THE TROUBLE began for Deepak Misra when he kissed his unattractive secretary in the office. But later he decided that the trouble had actually started some time before—around ten o'clock one morning when a friend called to tell him that his ex-wife Jill, who had left him a couple of years earlier and returned to her native Cleveland, was back in the city.

"Where?" Deepak asked, his voice tense.

"She's staying at the Annapurna Hotel. Says she's looking for an apartment."

"An apartment?"

"Looks as if she's here to stay, Deepak."

After he hung up, Deepak requested a file from his secretary, Bandana-ji, and asked her to wait while he scrutinized its contents. He thought of Jill's long face, the way her thin fingers, hovering over the canvas with a brush, gave the illusion that they were thinking. "My wife is back in Kathmandu," he said shortly. When Bandana-ji didn't respond, he looked up.

"Is there something wrong with the account?" she asked, pointing to the file.

"Just checking," he said, and handed it back to her.

Deepak had been a successful financial consultant for seven years. When Jill left him, everyone thought his business would collapse, that he'd plunge into something dark and horrible, probably aided by raksi, and his world would break apart. But Deepak showed remarkable endurance. Three days after Jill disappeared, without leaving even a note, he was back in the office, making phone calls, sending faxes, and tinkering with numbers on his new computer. Bandana-ji said, as if to the air in front of her, "It seems unnatural." She had been with him a little more than a year and was undiplomatic in her dealings with people. But Deepak liked her because she had a quick mind and a no-nonsense way about her that actually softened his clients. She was the best secretary he'd had.

Before Bandana-ji, there had been a young woman, Anju, who sat at her desk and combed her shiny, waist-long hair until it seemed to breathe. The floor beneath her desk and chair was always littered with strands of hair, and the janitor who came in every morning complained. Then when Anju started oiling her hair in the office, Deepak found smudges on important documents. Because her brother was his friend, he didn't fire her. Also—and Deepak admitted this to himself reluctantly — he found her pleasant to look at. When she lifted her mirror and studied her face or applied kazal to her eyes, he became entranced. But when more and more clients complained about important documents never reaching them or about incorrect calculations in their yearly assessments, Deepak had to let her go. He called her brother and apologized, to which her brother replied, "I'm surprised you kept her this long."

When he hired Bandana-ji, on the recommendation of a Marwari businessman, he was skeptical. The first time she entered his office, she cleared her throat so vigorously, the noise startled him. She also had an aloofness about her that disturbed

Deepak. She didn't appear comfortable around people, a draw-back in a secretary. On top of that, her thin hair was combed back with an awful-smelling oil, and she wore a purple sari with several patches. A prominent skin disfigurement on the right side of her face looked like a pink-colored map that started at the temple and curved down toward the chin. Later, Deepak thought it looked like a pregnant woman, whose protruding belly pointed toward Bandana-ji's nose. But her résumé was impeccable. She had worked for some of the top businessmen in the city, all of whom wrote laudatory recommendations. She even knew how to use a computer, a skill her previous em-ployer claimed she had learned on the job in a single day.

After her interview, when Deepak said he was interested in hiring her, she asked, in a coarse voice, "How much are you going to pay me?" When he told her, she smiled, scrunching up the pregnant woman's belly on her cheek, took her dilapidated folder from his desk, and walked out. He was stunned, but then he ran after her. She had already disappeared in the hustle and bustle of New Road outside his office. Two days later, he called her former employer and got her number. She answered the phone, and he quoted a higher salary. "That won't do," she said. Afraid she'd hang up, he asked what she expected. "Eight thousand rupees," she said, vigorously clearing her throat. He promptly agreed, though after he put the phone down, he won-dered why he'd given in to her exorbitant demand. She would be the highest paid secretary in the city. He could easily have hired another woman, perhaps equally competent, for half that salary.

When he reached the office the next morning, she was wait-ing outside the front door. "I need a key," she said, and he rushed to the key shop down the street to have one made. From then on, when he arrived at his office in the morning, she was there, and from the amount of work already accomplished, he knew she had been at her desk for at least an hour. The second day he made an extra cup of tea in his office and took it to her.

"I don't drink tea," she said, her eyes glued to the computer.

"Soft drink?" he asked.

"I don't drink soft drinks," she said.

He stood there, helpless, holding the cup of tea, staring at the hair on the back of her neck. She never drank or ate in the office, though she was there all day. A few days later he told her she should feel free to take an hour off for lunch, and if she brought lunch from home, she could put it in the fridge. He also recommended some restaurants down the street. "The Punjabi Restaurant has the best tandoori chicken in the city," he said.

"All right," she said.

When he came out of his office around lunchtime the following day to go for a walk and clear his mind of the numbers, she hadn't left her desk. "Make sure you lock the door when you go out for lunch," he said pointedly. She was still there when he returned.

Now, on this day, Deepak finished his work and went to the Annapurna Hotel. The receptionist checked the computer and said, "Yes, Jill Misra, Room 223." A small hope lit up inside Deepak—she'd kept his last name. He took the elevator upstairs and knocked on the door. There was no answer, so he went down and ordered a beer from the bar and let the cold seep into his stomach. He finished his beer in the lobby just as she walked in with a man. Deepak was about to call her name, but something stopped him. She had put on weight, and there was a glow to her face. The man with her was Nepali, thin and dark, and sporting a mustache that curved down to his chin. They walked past him and stepped into the elevator.

That night Deepak drank half a bottle of whiskey and listened to some ghazals—Urdu poems set to music—that he and Jill had loved during their three years of marriage. She likened the words of the ghazals, especially the surprise endings, to the strokes of her paintbrush. She had had her paintings exhibited in Kathmandu and Singapore, and before she left him, she had been trying to arrange shows in New Delhi and Bombay, cities with thriving artist communities.

Deepak got so drunk that the room began to spin. Deciding that he should eat something, he went to the kitchen to make an omelette, but soon became tired. An egg dropped from his hand and cracked on the floor, where the yolk spilled out, still intact, forming an eye. Deepak wished he had not fired his servant a few days ago, but the boy was lazy and had stolen money. Deepak staggered out of the house and, without thinking, got into his car. It was nearly ten o'clock, and the streets were abandoned. His car was weaving, but he didn't care, and he nearly hit a bicycle rider at the front corner of the Royal Palace.

At the Annapurna Hotel, he walked into the Chinese restaurant next to the lobby. It was empty, and he sat in a corner and ordered ginger chicken, which nauseated him after he'd taken a few bites. He wondered whether the mustached man was with Jill in her room or whether they had gone out. She liked to dance, so Deepak asked the waiter if there was a dance club in the hotel. On learning that there was, he went to the bathroom, washed his face, combed his hair, then stepped into the sparsely lit dance club. A deejay droned on about the "rhythm" of the forthcoming piece. Once Deepak's eyes adjusted to the light, he spotted Jill, standing at the edge of the dance floor, tapping her feet, a drink in her hand, and talking to the man with the ridiculous mustache.

"Welcome to Kathmandu," he said in English, awkwardly, when he reached them.

She looked at him not with surprise but amusement. "I had a feeling," she said in stilted Nepali. Her Nepali had been fluent when she left him. She introduced the mustached man as Birendra, and Deepak offered his hand.

"Well," she said.

Deepak went to the bar and ordered a drink, though he hardly took a sip after he went back to them. She was telling Birendra about an incident in Cleveland that involved a man and his dog. A thousand questions leaped to Deepak's mind. When she finished the story and Birendra laughed, Deepak grabbed her arm and said, "Just a moment." He led her to another corner of the dance floor, the revolving lights on the ceiling making her movements look jerky, and he stood there, not knowing what to say. She asked how he was, and he nodded, waved a hand in the air.

"You want an explanation," she said.

"Well, it is—"

"I have none," she said. She looked around the dance floor. "It just got to be too much. I had to get away. I guess we should file for divorce."

She was wearing a phuli on her nose, its diamond glittering, and her beauty stung him as it had when they first met, at a party. He recalled how his parents, who died soon after he married Jill, had advised him not to marry a foreigner. "You'll suffer later, son," his elderly mother had told him.

"We could," he told Jill now. He swallowed his drink in one shot and said, "What makes a woman leave her husband just like that? What had I done? No letter, no postcard. Nothing."

She stood there, holding her drink. "You knew I wasn't happy," she said.

He glanced at Birendra, who was staring in their direction. "Your friend," Deepak said.

"He's nothing," she said and asked Deepak whether he would drive her to the Swayambhunath Temple, a few miles away. She left without saying goodbye to Birendra.

In the car, she launched into a lengthy explanation about why she'd left him, but her words floated around him like a haze. He realized, now that she was here, that the question of why she had left him was no longer important, even though it had filled his mind so insistently during her absence. They climbed the steep steps to the temple, and, at the top, he kissed her. She pushed him away. In his drunkenness, he started to cry, and she held him, as one holds a weeping child. He told her that he was willing to forget what she had done to him, although he knew the alcohol was twisting his thoughts.

He wanted to take her home, but in the car she said that she wanted to "go slowly," and he accepted this, trying to envision a time when she would come back to him and everything would be as it was before.

"We should probably make today a holiday," he declared to Bandana-ji as he walked in.

"I have too much work to do," she said, without asking why he wanted a holiday. She rarely looked at him when she talked about subjects other than office matters. Deepak went to his room and called the hotel. The receptionist told him that Jill Misra was not in, so he left a message. Although there was much work to be done, his mind wandered. Through the glass partition, he saw Bandana-ji staring at the wall. Maybe she didn't feel well. She hadn't missed a day of work since she started. One Saturday afternoon, a few months after she joined him, he came to the office to fetch his address book and found

her at her desk, working. "I don't want you to work on a Saturday."

"Will you please just let me do my job?" Bandana-ji said
sternly.

"But you work—"

"I don't like people interfering with my work," Bandana-ji
said, as if he were an outsider.

He picked up his address book and walked out. She was a
strange creature. She never wore any sari other than the one she
had on when she came for her interview. Sometimes when he
was at his desk, he had the eerie sensation of being watched,
and when he looked up, he saw her quickly avert her eyes.

The next Saturday he had called the office just to check, and
her coarse voice answered, "Deepak Financial." He put the
phone down.

Now, watching her staring at the corner, Deepak called her
into his office and asked whether she was sick. "I feel fine," she
said.

"I saw you sitting still—"

"You want me to work like a slave?" She cleared her throat.

Deepak was taken aback. "No, I mean—"

"Did you see your wife? Is that why you are so perky?"

He looked closely at her face. Her eyes were small behind
her heavy glasses. He started to tell her about the night before,
but she interrupted him.

"What did she have to say?"

"Nothing," he said, suddenly unsure that he should be talking to her about Jill.

"These foreign women," Bandana-ji said, her face angry.

"She is just—"

"They think they can play with other people's lives." And she
went back to her desk.

Deepak was touched by her concern. She had never given an indication that she thought about Deepak's life outside the office, other than the one time she said, "It seems unnatural," when he came back to work the third day after Jill left. He thought, then, that she meant his returning to work so soon, but now it occurred to him that she may have been referring to Jill's abrupt departure.

His mind on Jill, Deepak didn't speak to Bandana-ji for the rest of the day. After work, he drove to the hotel, where the receptionist informed him that Jill had checked out an hour before. When Deepak asked whether she had left a forwarding address, the receptionist, a young man in an oversized suit, shook his head. "Did she get my message?" Deepak asked.

"She must have," the receptionist said. "There's nothing in her box."

For a few minutes, Deepak lingered in the lobby. He checked the restaurants, the dance club, the swimming pool, but Jill was nowhere.

He left the hotel and, leaving his car in the hotel parking lot, walked toward the area of Ghantaghar and Ranipokhari. Near the Ghantaghar clock tower, he saw students walk into Trichandra campus for their evening classes, the girls holding their notebooks close to their chests. The clock tower chimed six as he walked beneath it. At Ranipokhari he stood near the railings that surrounded the pond and stared down at the greenish murky water. He moved on to Asan, the bustling marketplace, and slipped into the crowd to distract himself from thinking about Jill.

As he passed a sari shop, he saw a reflection of Bandana-ji in one of its large mirrors. She was looking at the colorful saris laid out on the counter. Deepak stood still. She appraised a sari and bantered with the shopkeeper. Then she looked up and their eyes met in the mirror. Deepak wanted to pretend he hadn't seen her, but she was staring at him, so he stepped inside.

"Buying something?" he said.

"I'm trying to," she said, "but he's asking too high a price."

The sari was bright pink, with a delicate embroidery of flowers and hearts. A thin strip of velvet bound the edge.

"How much?" he asked the shopkeeper, who, on seeing a well-dressed man, became deferential. "Only three thousand rupees, sir," he said. "Discount price."

"Pack it up." Deepak reached into his pocket and gave him the money. He expected a strong protest from Bandana-ji, but she just stood there, clearing her throat.

They left the shop and moved toward Indrachowk as if they had planned this encounter. She walked with short, brisk steps, holding the bag with the sari and not looking at him. He found himself matching her steps. He knew she lived in the opposite direction, toward Baghbazar. They were repeatedly separated by other pedestrians, and every time they joined up again, Deepak had nothing to say. The sun, about to set, cast a pink glow on the buildings. The crowd thinned once they reached New Road, near his office, where Deepak felt compelled to say, "Where are you going?"

"You?"

"Just walking around." He told her he had left his car at the Annapurna Hotel.

"It's a beautiful evening," she said. She was attempting a smile.

"Are you going to wear that sari to the office?"

"You want me to?"

He nodded.

"Then I will."

Together, they went toward the office. Now she walked close

to him, the bag held to her chest, her shoulder occasionally touching his. He opened the door to the office and thought, This is crazy. Once inside, they immediately walked into his office. She looked at Jill's paintings on the wall as if she had never noticed them before. He sat in his chair and watched her.

"She's not that good," Bandana-ji said.

"She's talented."

She came to him and sat on his lap, still holding the bag. "Deepak Misra," she whispered. Deepak put his hand on her back. There wasn't enough flesh between each vertebra. He pulled her face toward him, kissed her on the lips, lightly, then with more force. His hand went to her breasts, so small that he could scarcely feel them. She responded with vigor, darting her tongue inside his mouth while her palms held his head. "Deepak Misra," she whispered again. When he found himself groping for the gap between her thighs, he became aware of the absurdity of the situation and gently pushed her aside. He opened a file and bent his head.

"You're thinking about her," she said accusingly.

"Who?" He brushed his hair with his fingers and sat up straight.

"Your American wife."

Deepak shook his head. "I'm going to leave now."

"She'll hurt you. You want that?"

"Bandana-ji," he said, "this is unbelievable. If you don't mind my saying so, it is none of your business."

She stood before him, her arms crossed over her scrawny chest. She started to speak, but when he said, "Don't," she stopped.

"I think of you all the time, Deepak Misra," she said softly.

Deepak, not knowing how to respond, smiled.

"I can give you much more than she will."

Deepak stepped toward the door, but she was in the way.
"I thought she had gone back to her country." Her small eyes
behind her glasses were filling with tears.

He put his hand on her shoulder. "This shouldn't have happened," he said. "You are my secretary."

On the drive home, Deepak was troubled by what he had done
with Bandana-ji. Now she was acting as if she were competing
with Jill.

Deepak took home some Chinese food and listened to the
sarod-playing of Amjad Ali Khan, another of Jill's favorites. She
was crazy about Indian classical music. When Deepak first met
her at the party, she had talked about how she loved Nepal and
India (Nepal more than India, she assured him), how she got
ideas for her paintings by just walking the streets of Kathmandu
and gazing at the carvings on the temples. Deepak had found
her charming, although she was like many of the Nepal-crazy
foreigners he knew, people who lived in the country in a romantic haze, love-struck by the mountain beauty and simple charms
of the people, but grossly naïve about their suffering.

Later during the party, he found her in an upstairs bedroom,
lying on the floor, her eyes closed, listening to the sitar-playing
of Ravi Shanker. There was something about her, the way her
blond hair fell about her face in disarray, the way her nose
twitched when the music took a turn, that made him sit beside
her and study her face. A while later she opened her eyes,
started to say something, then merely smiled at him.

After they were married, he discovered that she lived in a
space inside her mind that he could not reach. When they
returned from their honeymoon in Pokhara, she concentrated
so much on her painting that he believed she wouldn't even
notice if he left. At social gatherings, she mingled with other

guests with an ease that was alien to him. He had always been shy, and he felt abandoned when she left his side to talk with her friends. She became increasingly critical of his mannerisms, of his taste. "You didn't even smile at him when I introduced you," or "You call that a suit?" Her criticism hurt him, and before long he struck back, mocking her friends, calling them superficial, making negative comments about her paintings, criticizing her lack of cooking skill. He didn't want to, and he suffered pangs of self-loathing. So he began spending more time at work, for he loved her, and he couldn't abide the way she wounded him with her words. Often when he reached home at night, she was at a party. When she returned, she'd slip into bed without a word, and he was left staring at the ceiling. After a few months, she told him she was not happy. He held her, caressed her face, refusing to believe they couldn't be intimate again.

The morning she left, two years ago, he got up around six o'clock, just as the sun was rising, and saw the empty bed beside him. Although for the rest of the day he pretended that she was visiting friends, he knew that she had left him. What Deepak remembered most clearly about that morning was that the neighbor's cat, who always came into their house and cuddled up beside Jill, was sitting on the windowsill, staring at him, its green eyes eerie in the dim light. When he reached out to stroke its fur, it shrank back as if it were fearful of his touch.

"It's your wife," Bandana-ji said as she transferred the call.

"I need to talk to you," Jill said.

"What can I do for you?"

She told him she was coming over.

When she appeared at the door, Bandana-ji didn't look in her direction. Jill, wearing a sari, walked past Bandana-ji and said, "You're still working for him." Bandana-ji kept her eyes on the

computer screen. She hadn't yet worn the sari Deepak had
bought for her.

"Is she still strange?" Jill whispered as she sat in front of
Deepak.

He nodded. "Why didn't you tell me you were checking out
of the hotel?" She was wearing the gold necklace he'd given her
for their wedding. Her earlobes were weighted with heavy earrings, and she'd pulled her hair back so that her smooth cheeks
shone under the office lights.

"Didn't have time," she said. "Birendra offered me a room in
his apartment." She'd lost money in the casino, and now, since
she didn't want to stay with Birendra, she needed to borrow
money from Deepak.

"The house is still there," he said.

"I can't stay with you, Deepak."

Deepak went to the window. On the street below, two drivers
were arguing, and traffic had stalled. He knew she was using
him, yet he couldn't bring himself to say no. He opened the safe
in the corner, extracted ten thousand rupees, and handed them
to her.

"I'll return this soon."

He waved a hand in the air and became conscious that Bandana-ji was watching them through the glass. "Let's go for
lunch," he said to Jill.

They went to a nearby restaurant, and Jill told him that
Birendra wanted to sleep with her. "The other night he just
slipped into my bed," she said. "Nepali men, you know. Either
you're a mother, a sister, an aunt, or you're a whore."

Deepak laughed, and she, apparently pleased to see him
happy, laughed with him. Before they parted, he demanded she
promise to call him as soon as she found an apartment.

On his return to the office, he found the door locked. Inside, on Bandana-ji's desk, was a note: "I am not feeling well." Finally some time off, Deepak thought.

The next morning Bandana-ji came to the office wearing the pink sari and a matching pink blouse. "How different you look," he said. He wasn't sure someone so dark should wear such a light, buoyant color. He also noted a trace of lipstick on her lips, and was reminded of the story of the crow who wanted to become a swan.

Deepak asked her to stay after closing to finish some important documents that had to be mailed the next day. She came into his office, and they were cross-checking some numbers when he reached up and touched her lips. As the lipstick smudged his fingertips, he told her, "This color really suits you, Bandana-ji." She smiled, and suddenly Deepak felt his head become lighter. She bent toward him. "Deepak Misra," she whispered. "Every night in bed, you come and settle in my heart." They kissed, and his hands roamed her body. He unbuttoned her blouse, pushed up her bra, and began to suck her breasts. She helped him undress, and as he sat ridiculously naked on the Tibetan carpet, his penis firm and standing like the tower of Dharahara, she carefully took off her sari and petticoat but left her glasses on. She reminded him of a stork as she stood in front of him, her palms feebly covering her breasts. She smiled shyly, like a bride, and he felt a surge of happiness.

When he entered her, she kept repeating, "Oooohhhmmm," which sounded a lot like Om, the mantra for Lord Shiva, and it made him laugh, which made her laugh. Deepak's erection grew stronger by the minute. He was alive, as if the cells inside his body had awakened from sleep.

They had sex in the office once a week. Deepak became convinced that he had never before experienced such pleasure. Although sex with Jill had been satisfactory, she liked to talk about her paintings while he was inside her, and that bothered him. It excited her to talk like that, she said. But Bandana-ji gave him her complete attention, and the sweetness that entered his heart lasted for a couple of hours after they climaxed. They lay on the carpet, and she fell asleep, her head tucked neatly on his chest. Each time the pleasant feeling passed, however, and Deepak would get up abruptly, overcome by guilt and loathing. She would ask, "What happened?" and he would quietly put on his clothes and leave, without uttering a word.

For the few days between, they were boss and secretary again, but she came to be more and more beautiful to Deepak. Even the disfigurement on her face appeared to him a beauty mark, enhancing her appearance.

At Jill's housewarming party, Deepak sat with a glass of whiskey and watched Jill and Birendra whispering in the corner, like lovers. There were roughly a dozen people in the room, most of them expatriates working as artists or journalists in Kathmandu. Earlier, he had talked with a few of them, but he was bored with their incessant complaints about the Nepalese bureaucracy. When they went on like that, he wondered why they chose to live in a country they only found fault with.

Birendra was laughing at something Jill said, and, the whiskey warming his neck, Deepak walked over. They continued as if he weren't there.

"Excuse me," Deepak said. "May I talk to my wife alone?" He sounded belligerent, but he didn't care.

"Wife?" Jill laughed.

"We're not divorced yet," Deepak said.

Birendra looked at him with a smirk. "Deepak-ji, you're quite a man."

Deepak took a sip and glowered at Birendra, trying to think of something cutting to say.

"My Deepak," Jill said. "He's so sensitive. He should have

been the artist, not me." Today she was wearing a Punjabi salwar-kameez, and her dirty-blond hair spilled down her back.

"I must talk to you," he said.

"Okay." She walked out on the balcony, and he followed. The city lights spread out before them.

"How long are you going to continue with him?" he asked.

"Why do you want to know, Deepak Misra-ji?"

"Can't we—"

"It's hopeless, Deepak. You're insisting on something that's not possible."

"Why?" he said, his voice higher.

"There was a reason I left. We were both unhappy."

"Then why are you here?"

"You don't have a monopoly on this city," she said, throwing back her hair.

He was ashamed. They stood in silence for a while. Then she put her hand on his arm and said gently, "Let's go back inside."

Deepak left the party a short while later and wandered through the streets. His throat was parched from the alcohol. Then he started walking toward Baghbazar. The address was somewhere in the back of his mind, and he found the house, located off the main street. He stood in front of the three-story building, wondering whether he should knock on the bottom door, when he looked up and saw Bandana-ji in the second-floor window. Only her head and shoulders were visible, but he could see that she was wearing the pink sari and blouse. She glanced down and spotted him. When their eyes met, she stood still. She smiled, and he hurried away, his heart throbbing.

The next day Deepak decided that he couldn't go to the office. Over the phone he gave instructions to Bandana-ji, who didn't mention having seen him standing outside her apartment. For four days he stayed in bed until late in the morning, then got up and listened to music. In the evening he drank whiskey and walked around the house, looking at photographs of himself and Jill or of Jill alone. On the fourth afternoon, while he was listening to ghazals by Jagjit and Chitra Singh, the famous husband-and-wife singers, the doorbell rang. There was Bandana-ji, clutching some files. "I need your signature," she said.

As his sofa was piled up with his dirty clothes, something he kept telling himself to take care of, they sat on the living room carpet, where he signed the papers. It occurred to him he hadn't heard Bandana-ji clear her throat since they'd started making love. As he sat there, his head bent over the papers, she started to quietly sing along with Jagjit and Chitra Singh. She had a beautiful voice, and he stopped writing and listened. She smiled as she sang:

> If separated after meeting, we won't sleep at night.
> Thinking of each other, we'll cry at night.

He turned the volume down so that he could hear her more clearly. The words penetrated his skin, and he closed his eyes. When her voice went higher, he felt a shaft of pleasure enter his ears and run down his body. With his eyes closed, Deepak imagined the voice belonging to a different body, someone with a long neck, large deerlike eyes, and an aquiline nose. Then he imagined it belonging to Jill, and he saw her pale face as her tongue played with the words. Her hand reached out and caressed his face, then started unbuttoning his shirt. He opened his eyes and let Bandana-ji undress him. He undressed her, his throat dry with anticipation. She kept singing even when he entered her.

Deepak stayed in bed for days, sometimes reading, sometimes staring at the ceiling, often drifting into sleep. In the evening he got up, put on ghazals, and slowly drank himself into oblivion.

Every few days Bandana-ji came with papers for him to sign. Eventually he stopped asking questions about the office; he just took out his pen and signed what she handed him. Then he waited for her to sing. When he heard her voice, his body moved as though under a tender massage. The warmth spread from the bottom of his spine to the top of his head, and he arched his neck to hold on to the sensation.

The phone rang constantly. People buzzed the doorbell and knocked loudly. Once he heard Jill calling, "Deepak, what's the matter? Open up." But he opened the door only for Bandana-ji, after peering through the curtains to make sure it was she. When she told him that some clients were irritated by his absence, he said, "Tell them I've gone to Singapore for a conference." And when he finished his stock of whiskey, he drove to a nearby shop and bought two cases. Every hour without Bandana-ji was a long stretch of boredom, and he constantly thought of the pregnant woman on her face, the bones of her hips.

One afternoon, with Bandana-ji on top of him on the carpet, humming, Deepak saw someone move past the window curtains toward the back of the house. There was a creak, and he knew that someone had opened the back door, which he had forgotten to lock the night before. He recognized the footsteps as Jill's. Then Deepak saw her legs at the entrance of the living room, and looked at Bandana-ji. Although her eyes were closed, Deepak knew that she was aware of Jill's presence. What a sight, Deepak thought: the whole house smelling of alcohol, and he, on the carpet, straddled by Bandana-ji. Deepak moaned, and their movement became quicker until they climaxed. As Bandana-ji's head came to rest on his chest, Deepak turned his head and saw the empty space where Jill had been a moment ago.

His pleasure was mixed with a strange satisfaction, as if he had won a battle he'd been fighting for days. But that didn't last long. After Bandana-ji left, he became filled with self-loathing. He drank so much that he bumped into tables and lamps. In the living room he picked up a large photograph of Jill and, after glancing at it briefly, set it back, face down. He did the same with other pictures of her. He felt Jill was laughing at him.

Despite all the whiskey, Deepak couldn't sleep. In the middle of the night he got up and took a cold shower, made himself a cup of tea, and sat in the living room, looking out the window into the darkness. He could hear the frogs outside, and their melodic croaking calmed his nerves. As the darkness gave way to a gray light, and the birds started chirping, his head cleared, and he reached a decision, a painful one.

The next day, his body tired but his mind fresh, Deepak asked Bandana-ji to submit her resignation. She didn't protest. She went to her desk, entered something into the computer, and came back into his office. He had a stack of money in front of him, much more than what he owed her, but she carefully counted the money and took only what was due her. He wanted to say that he was sorry, but the only thing he could do was stare at the rest of the money on the desk.

It took him less than a week to hire another secretary, a short older woman with a loud voice. She wasn't as efficient as Bandana-ji, but she caught on fast, and her phone manner was impeccable for someone with such a booming voice. For about a week, Deepak's life acquired a semblance of normality again. The pleasure he had experienced with Bandana-ji now seemed unreal.

But this sense of control soon gave way to restlessness, a feeling of emptiness. He began to compare his current state to the rapture he had experienced when Bandana-ji sang to him. His everyday life was so lacking in color that he worried that something had happened to his brain. When he went to Jill's apartment for another party, this time a celebration of a solo exhibition in the city, she was no longer attractive to him. He wondered why he had so desperately wanted her back in his life. It was evident that Jill and Birendra were lovers now, for they held hands throughout the party, their bodies close to each other.

One afternoon, a small boy delivered a package to Deepak at the office, and in it he discovered the pink sari. He picked it up and smelled it. It no longer bore her smell, that odor of cooking oil, so he assumed it had been cleaned. After work, he drove to Baghbazar and, with the package in his hand, knocked on the bottom door. An old lady told him that Bandana-ji had moved out, and that an Indian family now lived in her flat. No, she didn't know where Bandana-ji had gone. The old lady shook her head, revealing toothless gums as she smiled. "She was a strange one," she said. "She didn't talk to anyone." She paused, and a wistful look came over her face. "But she sang beautifully. It can only be God's blessing."

It was getting dark. Deepak decided to leave his car and walk around the block. There were many sari shops in the area, and he peered into each one as he walked past, the pink sari package in his hand, with the absurd hope that Bandana-ji might be buying another. The street was half-lit with shoplights, as there were no street lamps above. Whenever he saw a thin woman in a shop, he stopped to see whether it was Bandana-ji. At one point, he heard a woman clear her throat, and followed her for a short distance.

He walked the streets until he lost his bearings. His fingers were moist from clutching the package. By this time many shopkeepers had closed their doors and turned off the lights. After about an hour, he realized that he had walked all the way to Kupondole, past the Bagmati Bridge, which separated the cities of Kathmandu and Patan. He sat on the steps of a closed shop near a bus stop and listened to music coming from a stereo shop around the corner. Soon he recognized the voices of Jagjit Singh and Chitra Singh, and he walked to the shop. A small man inside smiled at him. Deepak stood outside, listening.

> This night I have to stay awake till dawn:
> My fate is etched like this.
> Sorrow has entered my heart.
> Stars, why don't you fall asleep?

He closed his eyes, and in a moment he realized the voice he was hearing was Bandana-ji's, not those of the famous singers. And he saw her face, the pregnant woman on her cheek. Arching his neck, Deepak waited for the sensation of bliss to enter his body.

The Limping Bride

"GET HIM MARRIED," Rudra said. "Once he has a wife, he'll come to his senses."

"Who'd marry him?" Hiralal said. "The whole city knows he's a drunkard."

They were smoking, sitting in Rudra's rice-and-beans shop in the neighborhood. Hiralal dragged on his Yak cigarette, and Rudra smoked from the chilim, making gurgling sounds as he sucked on the long thin pipe. Hiralal and Rudra had grown up in the same neighborhood, attended the same school a few blocks away, and had teased the same girls. Over the years, as his business prospered, Rudra had grown fat, and now he sat in his shop all day, groaning whenever he had to get up to scoop rice for a customer.

"We'll find someone," he said.

"I don't know," Hiralal replied. The sun was setting, and he could hear voices haggling at the nearby vegetable market. It was always in the evening that Hiralal most missed Rammaya. From his window he'd see her in the courtyard, combing her long black hair under the mild winter sun. She'd tilt her head as she combed the coconut-scented Dabur Anwla oil through her hair. Occasionally she'd look up at him, and he'd say something like, "Aren't you going to come up?" She'd shake her head and go back to her combing. When she did finally come upstairs, he'd hover around her, just to smell her hair.

A woman came in to buy some mung beans, and after she left, Rudra said, "Why don't I ask my wife to find someone? Anyone. I think the important thing is to get him married."

Hiralal knew what Rudra meant by "anyone." It meant they'd have to find a girl with a blemish on her face, one with pockmarks, a girl whose parents wouldn't mind giving her away in haste — even to a drunkard. But Moti was getting out of control. Hiralal could imagine Moti lying on the street, face down, a patch of blood and vomit next to his head. He didn't know where Moti found the money for his drinking; he probably relied on friends, sons of local merchants. Perhaps he even borrowed money from them. Moti had held a few jobs, mostly menial, but never for long; either his employers fired him or he simply stopped going to work. Now, at nineteen, he staggered through the streets, his eyes red and puffy, speaking to strangers in a slurred voice, stumbling into the alleys of Jaisideval whenever he came across his father.

Hiralal said okay to Rudra.

The drinking had begun when Moti was seventeen. He stayed out late and came home with alcohol on his breath. At first, Hiralal and Rammaya merely scolded him. But when he took up drinking in the afternoon, Hiralal had had enough. One evening when Moti arrived home swaying and staggering, Hiralal cut a branch from a tree in the garden and whacked his son's legs. "You think you're a big man."

Rammaya, cooking in the kitchen, rushed down the stairs and stood in front of Moti, her arms outstretched. "Don't you dare hit our son," she told Hiralal. Their first child had died of pneumonia when she was six months old, which propelled Rammaya into a depression that lifted only when Moti was born. "You hit him again," Rammaya had told Hiralal, "and I will leave you."

For two days Moti stayed home, teetering around the house, a surly expression on his face whenever he ran into his father. Then, once he was steady on his feet, he returned to the neighborhood bhatti, a dark bar with tables and benches and a counter displaying fly-infested meat snacks. Hiralal and Rammaya tried talking to him calmly, and Moti listened, sometimes nodding, sometimes raising his eyes—large, like his mother's —to look at his parents. "Do you promise not to drink?" Hiralal asked his son, and Moti said, "I promise." Later that night, in bed, Rammaya said, "He won't do it again. I know my son." But the next day, after work, Hiralal peered into the bhatti, and there was Moti, his head against the wall, his eyes closed. As Hiralal stood in the doorway, the anger rising inside him, one of Moti's friends nudged the boy. He opened his eyes, saw his father, and scrambled to get up, spilling the glass of raksi in front of him. Swaying as he stood, he said, "Ba?" as if he were asking Hiralal a question. Hiralal grabbed him by the right ear, and dragged him home, not saying a word, ignoring the looks of the pedestrians who stopped to see what was happening. At home, he took Moti to Rammaya in the kitchen, and said, "You said you knew your son."

When it became clear that Moti would not stop drinking, Rammaya again became depressed. Hiralal did not understand why Moti drank, and asked himself whether Moti felt something absent from his life. Both Hiralal and Rammaya had doted on their son. It occurred to Hiralal that perhaps that was the problem: perhaps they had pampered him. They were never able to say no to him, even when he demanded things they could barely afford: a large toy ship when he was seven, a brand-new Chinese bicycle when he was twelve, a trip to the Indian border to watch movies with his friends when he was fifteen. If Moti didn't get what he wanted, he threw a fit, and Hiralal and Rammaya would succumb. Their giving in to their son's every demand, Hiralal now thought, had turned Moti into a needy teenager, someone who felt insecure when faced with the rejections and disappointments of the larger world. Even as a teenager Moti had clung to Rammaya and sought her protection when he couldn't deal with his father's anger.

"It's not our fault," Hiralal told Rammaya. "People do what's etched on their foreheads at birth." He enumerated for her the children from good families who'd gone astray: his cousin Bhola's young daughter, who had eloped with a truck driver; their neighbor Hom's son, who languished in jail for the murder of a police inspector; Rammaya's own niece, who was rumored to be working as a prostitute in the city's luxury hotels.

But Rammaya could not be consoled. She moved around the house slowly and took longer to do her household duties. In bed, she hardly spoke to Hiralal, and sometimes when he woke in the middle of the night, he found her sitting, staring up at the ceiling.

One morning she complained of a headache, and within a week she was gone. "Meningitis," the doctors said. It was as if someone had sucked the breath right out of Hiralal's body. And no tears came. He tried to cry, but his eyes only burned.

After Rammaya's ashes floated away on the Bagmati River, Moti's drinking became worse. He went to the bhatti in the morning and stayed until it closed. Sometimes Hiralal heard him crying in his room. One morning Hiralal went to him and asked, "You miss your mother?"

Moti looked at his father with cloudy eyes and said, "Ma comes to me in my dreams."

Hiralal smiled. "She never comes to me. She must love you more than she loves me." All day long it bothered him that he hadn't dreamed of Rammaya since she died.

A week later, Rudra's wife offered a proposal. A beautiful girl's parents were looking for a groom for their daughter. Hiralal waited for the bad news. "She has a slight limp in her left leg," Rudra's wife said. Hiralal sighed. This was not what he had imagined for his son. "But she's very beautiful," Rudra's wife added. "And a very good girl. She'll take care of Moti. Bring him around."

Hiralal looked at the framed picture of Rammaya by his bedside. Would she have even considered this? "Moti has to agree," he said to Rudra's wife. "Do the girls' parents —?"

"They know," she said. "But they're anxious to find someone for their daughter." Before leaving, she told Hiralal, "I'll bring a photograph tomorrow. The parents were unwilling to give me a picture unless you were interested."

Hiralal was grateful to her for acting as a lami—the middle woman—for Moti, but he felt bad for the girl's parents, having to settle for their daughter's marrying a drunkard. But what else could they do? Let their daughter be mocked by neighbors and relatives all through her life? Hiralal knew how his society viewed such matters: better to have an alcoholic son-in-law than no son-in-law.

The next morning, after getting dressed for work, Hiralal went to Moti's room and had to shake his son a few times before he opened his eyes.

"There's a proposal for you," Hiralal said.

Moti sunk his face in the pillow. "Ba, I'm sleeping."

"A beautiful girl. From a very good family."

Moti turned his head. "What are you talking about?"

"I'm saying that you should get married. And we've found the right girl for you."

Moti laughed. "Where's this talk coming from?"

Hiralal didn't know how to answer. "Is this how you're going to spend your life? Getting drunk, no job, no school?"

"Please, Ba, I have a headache."

"Oh, really? I wonder why."

Moti again buried his face in the pillow.

"I'll arrange for a viewing."

"Do what you want," Moti said in a muffled voice. "I'm not getting married."

"We'll see about that."

On the bus to Jawalakhel, Hiralal puzzled over how to persuade Moti to come to the viewing. Over the past months, Hiralal had been remembering how, as a child, Moti liked to tour the city with him on Saturdays. They'd go to Patan, stroll in the square, with its intricately carved temples and the curio shops where foreigners bought small replicas of city monuments. They'd go to the Balaju Garden, with its twenty-two stone spouts gushing water, watch men bathe in their white underwear, women wash gigantic mounds of clothes. In Budhanilkantha, at the northern edge of the valley, they'd circle the huge statue of Vishnu reclining on a bed of snakes. Moti's favorite place was the Swayambhunath Temple, perched on a hillock to the west. They would climb a steep staircase to the top, and Hiralal would have trouble catching up to Moti, who'd bound up the stairs like one of the hundreds of monkeys that roamed the temple complex. When they reached the top, Moti's face would be flushed, and he'd rush to the lookout that opened on a breathtaking view of the valley. Moti loved to identify the city landmarks: the royal palace, with its strange curves; the large Tundikhel field, which now looked like a small green patch between the buildings; the Dharahara tower, standing like a white pencil. "Our house is there," Moti would say, his finger struggling to pinpoint the exact location of Jaisideval in the cluster of houses far away.

Hiralal worked as a driver for a rich Marwari businessman, Chaudhari saheb, who owned shops and restaurants in the city and two distilleries in the outskirts of the valley. Hiralal had been working for him for nearly twenty-five years, shuttling Chaudhari saheb in a Toyota Corolla between his shops and factories. Chaudhari saheb had treated Hiralal well, giving him bonuses during the Dashain Festival and the New Year, but he had one habit that annoyed Hiralal: he was a back-seat driver. When Hiralal became really annoyed, he would say, "I've been driving for years, hujoor." Chaudhari saheb would grimace and say, "That doesn't mean you don't have to be careful."

This evening Hiralal was tired. In Thapathali, Chaudhari saheb had shouted, "A bus to your right," directly into Hiralal's ear, making his head ring. Later, when Hiralal swerved too close to another car, Chaudhari saheb let out a series of grunts, like an animal. Hiralal had half a mind to stop the car and ask Chaudhari saheb to drive while he sat back and offered advice. As it was, driving in Kathmandu had become increasingly nerve-wracking. Hiralal was always having to avoid ricksaw-pullers, pedestrians who crossed the street with abandon, reckless taxis, bus drivers who smirked as they tried to run him off the road, government cars that cruised as if they owned the road, and village idiots who waited until the last possible minute to jump in front of him.

But Hiralal's exhaustion vanished when Rudra's wife came to his house to show him the picture of the girl. She was indeed beautiful, with large, kind eyes and a slim nose. "She looks like a good girl," he said to Rudra's wife, who responded, "She's a very good girl." She was a year younger than Moti, she added, and a perfect match. "Of course, you'll have to drive it into his head that his old ways cannot continue, or the girl's life will be destroyed."

Hiralal debated whether to tell Rudra's wife that Moti still needed to be convinced. But she might take that for a no and stop the negotiations. After all, her reputation as the middle woman was at stake. "He'll come around," Hiralal said, and kept the photograph to show to Moti.

Late that night when Moti came home, Hiralal took a plate of dal-bhat to his room.

"I'm not hungry," Moti said. He was struggling to get into his pajamas. The room reeked of cheap liquor.

"You have to eat something. With all that drinking—"

"Ba, I already ate." He sat on the bed.

Hiralal sat beside him and held up the picture. "Here, take a look."

Moti gave his father a quizzical glance and then laughed. "You don't give up, do you? I told you."

"Just take a look."

Moti nodded at the picture and said, "No."

"Look closely. See how beautiful she is."

"Ba . . ." Moti started to say something, then took the picture and peered at it. Hiralal, watching his face closely, thought Moti's drunken eyes lit up. "She's okay," Moti said after a moment.

"So, I'll arrange for a viewing?"

"As I said before, I'm not getting married. I'll go for your sake, but I won't marry her."

Hiralal put his arm around Moti. "Son, she's a good girl. You'll get married, get a job, I'll have grandchildren."

Moti chuckled. "I'm just nineteen, Ba. What will I do with a wife? Just produce grandchildren for you?"

"What's the harm in looking? If you don't like her, you'll say no."

Moti leaned back on his elbows.

"Think of your mother," Hiralal said. "This is what she'd have wanted."

After a moment, Moti said, "All right, I'll look. But I'm warning you, be prepared for a no."

Hiralal left the picture by the bedside.

He couldn't sleep that night. This was the girl meant for Moti. After he saw her sweet face, Moti would change his ways. At two o'clock, Hiralal turned on the light and looked at the framed photograph of Rammaya hanging on the wall next to the bed. She was wearing a traditional Nepali shawl, the khasto, her broad face smiling at the camera, her hand holding the brass plate she used when she went to a temple, her forehead marked with vermilion paste. Hiralal remembered when the picture was taken. She had just come back from the Kathmandu Geneshthan, the temple of the elephant god, only a short distance from their house, and Moti, then sixteen, asked her to pose in front of the garden in the courtyard. A few weeks before, Moti had seen the camera in a shop and had relentlessly pestered Hiralal to buy it for him. When Hiralal pointed out that it cost three thousand rupees, an entire month's salary, Moti went to his room and slammed the door. When he didn't eat for two days, Rammaya sold her gold ring and handed the money to Hiralal. She refused to listen to his objection and said, "He's our only son."

Hiralal watched as Rammaya stood next to the white roses and complained as Moti asked her to move this way and that. Moti said, "Smile," in English, as if he were one of the foreigners who clicked cameras in the nearby Durbar Square temples. When Rammaya smiled, Hiralal couldn't help smiling himself.

★

Hiralal, Moti, and Rammaya's uncle, an old man with a stoop, went to the girl's house for the viewing. She was seated, Hiralal noted with relief when they entered the living room.

A servant brought tea and biscuits, and the girl's father, a large man with a paunch, said, "Rukmini is our only child."

Hiralal nodded. "Moti is my only son. Our first child, a daughter, died when she was a child."

They chatted for a while, and eventually Rukmini's father said, "Well, I expect Moti babu will get a job once they're married."

"Of course, of course," Hiralal said. Moti was wearing a suit and had combed his hair, and Hiralal thought he looked handsome except for his eyes, ravaged by all that drinking. Hiralal had pleaded with him not to drink on this important morning, and to his surprise Moti had complied.

Moti stole glances at Rukmini, who sat beside her mother on the sofa, her eyes focused on the floor. She was wearing a pink sari and matching pink lipstick. Once she briefly lifted her head to catch a glimpse of Moti, and then looked down again. Hiralal noticed that her legs were covered by her sari.

When they were about to leave, Moti abruptly said, as if to the air in front of him, "It would be good if she and I could talk. Alone."

The room became silent.

"This is not normally done," Rukmini's father said.

Hiralal, though surprised by Moti's request, said, "What harm will it do? Just for a short time."

Rukmini's father looked at his wife, who nodded. The parents went to the next room, where they waited impatiently, the girl's father frequently glancing toward the door. After about ten minutes, Moti came out, his face slightly flushed. "Let's go," he said to Hiralal.

"So, what is the decision?" the girl's father asked.

Hiralal was about to say that he'd get back to him tomorrow when Moti said, "Yes."

All eyes were on him.

"Everything is all right, then?" Hiralal asked.

Moti nodded.

In the taxi, Hiralal said, "What did you talk about?"

"This and that." Moti was still avoiding his father's eyes, as if he were embarrassed.

"Did she get up to see you off at the door?"

"Why?"

"Just asking, wondering what happened." Hiralal's heart was beating rapidly. He didn't want to push this, lest Moti change his mind.

"So what did you like about her, Moti?" Rammaya's uncle said with a laugh. "I thought you were not going to marry."

Moti smiled.

Hiralal nudged Rammaya's uncle to query Moti further.

"So, what is it? What about her?"

"She reminds me of—" Moti turned red and shook his head.

"Who?" Hiralal asked.

But Moti, looking out the window, didn't answer.

During the next few days, Hiralal was beset with anxiety. Every time Moti came home, Hiralal expected him to fly into a rage. To say he'd learned about her limp through someone—a friend, a relative, a stranger who'd whispered to him on the street, "The girl is a langadi." But Moti apparently hadn't heard.

As the day of the wedding approached, Hiralal couldn't sleep. Once or twice he almost got up and went to tell Moti the truth. But the wedding was already set. Moti was sure to rebel, and the family's name would be destroyed forever. Rukmini's father would be humiliated among his relatives and neighbors, and the poor girl would have an even tougher time getting married. When Hiralal did manage to doze off, he woke instantly to his own voice. He suspected he was saying Rammaya's name.

On the big day, Moti was dressed in a smart brown suit tailored for the wedding. He had even borrowed cologne from his friend —to hide the stench from his mouth, Hiralal was certain—and a faint aroma of musk hovered around him. Surprisingly, Moti was steady in his movements, and he joked with his friends and chatted with relatives.

The wedding procession marched to the bride's house, where the ceremony began. Rukmini, dressed in a red sari, golden jewelry shining on her neck and ears, was led to the garden by her mother and aunts. They seemed to be lifting her with their arms so that her limp wouldn't show, and for a moment Hiralal forgot that his daughter-in-law was a langadi. He hated that ugly word anyway; it reduced this beautiful girl's entire existence to her limp. Under a canopy, the bride and groom were seated side by side, and the priests started chanting. After an hour, it began to rain, first small drops, then a torrent, which sent the guests scurrying to the large tent in a corner of the compound. "Rain means there's blessing from above," people commented. Hiralal held his breath as Rukmini and Moti circled the wedding pyre, but they were moving so slowly, and there were so many umbrellas in the way, that Rukmini's limp was obscured. At one point Hiralal overheard two women whispering that Moti wasn't aware the girl was a langadi, but they stopped when Hiralal glared at them.

Hiralal had managed to borrow Chaudhari saheb's Toyota Corolla for the day, so the bride and the groom rode in the back seat while a procession of cars, taxis, and motorcycles followed them toward the groom's house.

Hiralal's aunt ushered Rukmini into the house and then into

Moti's room, where she was introduced to all the members of her husband's extended family, one by one. She knelt before them and touched their feet.

After the introductions, the relatives left, and Rukmini was alone. Moti was in Hiralal's room, talking with his friends, who also soon took their leave. Hiralal hovered between the two rooms, then peeked into the room where Rukmini sat on the bed, head down, and told her, "If you need anything, I'm in the other room." He paused. "Anything." He went to his own room, where Moti was lying on the bed, his eyes closed. "Tired?" Hiralal asked. Moti nodded without opening his eyes. "Well, there's someone waiting for you," Hiralal said. Moti got up and went to his bride.

Hiralal changed, then sat on his bed. It had been a long day, but his heart was beating so rapidly, he knew there would be no sleep. He lay down and stared at the ceiling, trying to hear sounds from the other room. He could hear Moti murmuring, but he couldn't make out the words. Would Moti notice her limp now? Hiralal didn't even know how bad it was. Was one of her knees twisted? Was one leg shorter than the other? He should have asked Rudra's wife.

He must have fallen asleep, because he woke to a loud slam of the downstairs door. He quickly went to the window and saw Moti heading out of the courtyard to the street. He looked into Moti's room and saw Rukmini sitting on the bed, crying. "What happened?" he asked.

She kept crying.

Hiralal sat beside her and put his arm around her shoulder. She looked up at him, the kohl on her eyes running down her cheeks. "He didn't know?" she asked.

Hiralal shook his head.

"How could you do this?" she said. "He told me he wasn't going to stay with me."

"He will," Hiralal said, unsure. "He will accept it. He's lucky to have someone like you."

"First, I get married to a drunkard," she said between sobs. "Then, he calls me a langadi and walks out. On my wedding day."

He tried to console her, saying that Moti's rage was only temporary, that he'd appreciate her once he got to know her. When she became quiet, he told her, aware of the absurdity of his words, "Try to get a good night's sleep," and left her to her misery.

It was midnight. Hiralal changed into his trousers and walked out of the house.

The street was deserted. A few houses away, he came across a group of young boys loitering outside a closed shop. One was Moti's friend who had attended the wedding. Without being asked, the friend said, "Moti bought a bottle of raksi here and went, I don't know where." Hiralal nodded at the boys and left.

He found Moti on top of the platform of the Shiva-Parvati Temple in the Durbar Square, a block away. Moti, in his pajamas, was drinking straight from the bottle. When he saw his father, he said, "Bastard. Betrayer."

Hiralal tried to touch him, but Moti slapped his hand and moved away, taking another swig from the bottle.

"I didn't do this because I wanted to, Moti," Hiralal said.

"I am not going to stay with her." His speech was slurred.

"You have to," Hiralal said. "She's your wife now."

Moti got up and said loudly, "Motherfucker. Why don't you take her as your wife?"

"Moti."

"Fuck Moti." Spittle appeared on his lips.

Hiralal tried to grab the bottle, but Moti held it tight and tried to hit his father. Hiralal slapped him, hard, on the right cheek.

"Motherfucker," Moti said again. "You've ruined my life."

"You're a drunkard. You're lucky to have someone like her."

Moti sat down again on the platform and started crying, saying "Ma" and repeating, "You've ruined my life."

"Let's go back."

It took a while, but Hiralal managed to coax Moti into returning home. He still held the bottle, taking a swig every now and then, his cheeks wet with tears. When the two came across his friends, Moti shouted, "My wife is a langadi." The boys stared at the father and son.

On the staircase, Hiralal succeeded in prying the bottle from him. Moti could hardly stand up, and he was mumbling more obscenities. Hiralal led him to his room, where Rukmini sat in the same position as when he had left her. When she saw Moti in his drunken state, she turned her face away. Moti said, "I'm not sleeping here," and struggled away from his father to lurch into the kitchen, where he crashed to the floor. Hiralal told Rukmini, "He'll come around. Not to worry." Grabbing a blanket from his room, he took it to the kitchen, where Moti was lying face down, and placed it over his son.

In the morning, Hiralal woke to sounds in the kitchen. Soon Rukmini appeared, the edge of her dhoti covering her hair, a glass of tea in her hand, the bangles on her wrist jingling as she set the tea on the table. In the light of the morning, Hiralal saw her face clearly for the first time, and was struck, once again, by her beauty. Why would God curse such a beautiful girl with a lame foot?

"Would you like something to eat?" she asked. Her voice was low and sad. "Shall I boil an egg?"

He shook his head. "Is Moti still sleeping?"

She nodded.

He wanted to comfort her, tell her his son was not a bad boy.

But she had spent the first night of her married life alone while her husband lay, drunk, on the kitchen floor.

As she walked away, he saw that her limp was quite pronounced; she had to hobble to make her shorter foot touch the floor.

Moti came home drunk every night and slept on the kitchen floor. He didn't speak to Hiralal, and he didn't utter a word to his new wife. When he woke in the morning to the sounds of Rukmini cooking and cleaning, he abruptly got up and went to the bathroom. He washed himself, changed, and left the house. At around nine o'clock, Hiralal ate in the kitchen as Rukmini sat in front of him, ready to serve more lentils or vegetables. "Why don't you eat with me?" he once asked her, but she said, "I'll eat after you leave." He wondered whether she thought about going back to her parents. If she did, she gave no indication. She worked around the house—cooking, cleaning, not speaking unless spoken to. One morning, just as Moti was coming out of the bathroom, Hiralal said, "How long will this go on? How long are you going to treat her this way?"

Moti said, "You have no right to speak to me," and pushed past him to his room.

At work, Hiralal found himself wondering what his daughter-in-law was doing. One afternoon, after dropping off some documents at a branch office in New Road, Hiralal drove to Jaisideval. That morning Chaudhari saheb had taken ill, so Hiralal had some free time. As he entered his courtyard, he saw Rukmini, seated on Rammaya's straw mat in a patch of sunlight, combing her hair. Hiralal stopped. Rukmini's comb was black, not yellow like Rammaya's, but she, too, tilted her head as she ran the comb through her hair in long strokes. When she saw Hiralal, she abruptly tied back her hair, stood, and went inside. He followed. As she hobbled up the staircase, he sniffed the air behind her, but apparently she didn't use coconut oil. She walked into the kitchen, and he went to his room, sat on the bed, and looked at the floor. When at last he came out, he ran into her just outside the door, holding a glass of tea. "I have to leave," he told her, and she said, "But I just made tea." He glanced at his wristwatch and saw that he had a few minutes before he was scheduled to pick up Chaudhari saheb's son from school.

He took the tea from her and went to the kitchen, where he sat down on a pirka and started sipping. "And you?" he asked. She poured tea for herself and sat on her haunches in front of him. They both sipped, Hiralal making loud noises, while hardly a sound came from her lips. He stole glances at her face, trying to figure out what she was thinking, but she concentrated on the tea. He knew Rammaya would have liked her, the way her soft voice sounded, the way her eyes gently took in her surroundings, the way she moved gracefully around the house, even with her limp.

"Would you like bread?" she asked.

"I don't have time," he said, finishing his tea. "I have to leave now."

She stood at the top of the stairs and watched as he walked down. At the bottom he turned back, and she asked, "You'll come home at the same time as usual?"

He nodded.

The next day, since Chadhari saheb was still sick, Hiralal went home in the afternoon, and Rukmini, as if she'd been expecting him, had already poured milk and sugar into the kettle. Again, he sat on the pirka, and they drank their tea. She asked whether he wanted anything to eat, and he said no. She stood at the top of the stairs, and he turned back at the bottom before he left. The routine continued for several days; as long as Chaudhari saheb was bed-ridden, Hiralal always found an excuse to drop by the house. When he arrived home in the evening, it was as if nothing had happened in the afternoon. She stayed in the kitchen, cooking the evening meal, and he joined her when the food was ready. After he ate, he went to his room, chewed on a betel nut, and smoked a cigarette, while she ate by herself and then washed the dishes. Moti, who never came home in the afternoon, swaggered in late at night from the bhatti and slept on the kitchen floor, sometimes after eating the dinner she had left him on a plate, sometimes without touching it.

One afternoon, while Rukmini and Hiralal were drinking tea, Moti appeared at the kitchen door, swaying like a bamboo pole in a breeze. He said to his father, "How come you're home?"

"I was in the area."

Moti's forehead creased. He left the kitchen but reappeared a few minutes later, as Hiralal was washing his mouth. "Get dressed," he told Rukmini. "We're going to the cinema."

Hiralal wiped his hands and mouth with a towel, careful not to show his surprise. "Go ahead," he said to Rukmini, who was watching Moti.

"Quick," Moti said harshly. "We'll miss the three o'clock show."

Rukmini went to change her clothes.

"You need money?" Hiralal asked Moti.

"I don't need your money."

Hiralal fished in his pocket and took out a hundred-rupee note. "Here, take her to a nice restaurant."

Moti said, "I'll take care of my own wife. I don't need your help."

Rukmini came back, wearing the pink sari and pink lipstick

she'd worn when they'd first met her, as well as long golden earrings.

"Why don't I drop you two at the cinema?" Hiralal said. "The car is right outside."

"We'll take a taxi," Moti said.

Rukmini said, "But a taxi will be expensive. Ba's car is right here."

"I have the money," Moti said.

The three walked outside together. On the street, Hiralal got into the car, and Moti and Rukmini began walking toward Basantapur. Moti stayed slightly ahead of her, and Hiralal watched her limp after him. He started the car and waited for her to look back at him, but she was concentrating on catching up with her husband. Hiralal turned the car around.

That evening, alone at home, Hiralal sat by the window overlooking the street. It was already dark outside, and the shops and houses had their lights on. He wasn't hungry, even though it was past his usual dinner hour. He watched the passersby below, cyclists with their dim lights, and farmers shuffling down the street with their baskets swinging from the poles on their shoulders. He knew he should be thinking of Rammaya, missing her, but this evening he couldn't even summon up her face. There she was, in the framed picture on the wall, with a smile. Her eyes seemed to be judging him critically. He moved from the window to the door, and her eyes followed him. Hiralal left the room and went down to the courtyard, where he could feel a breeze across his face.

A few minutes later, Rudra passed by, twirling his shop keys on his finger. "What's happening, Hiralal?" he said jovially. "Looks as if Moti has finally taken a fancy to his wife." He'd seen them get into a taxi in front of his shop. "I told you he'd come around."

After he left, Hiralal waited outside for nearly an hour, but his legs grew tired, so he went to the kitchen and sat on the pirka. He didn't want to go to his room and face Rammaya's critical eyes. How could he explain to his dead wife how he felt toward his daughter-in-law? A tremendous feeling of guilt washed over him. He could smell Rukmini in the kitchen, the faint whiff of onions and body oil. He went to Moti's room and turned on the light. Rukmini's dhoti lay on the bed, crumpled, part of it spilling to the floor. Hiralal knelt down and smelled it. Yes, it had her smell. He pulled the dhoti to his face and rubbed it against his cheeks.

Downstairs, there was laughter. Hiralal turned off the light and stood at the top of the stairs, watching Rukmini hold Moti's arm as he stumbled up drunkenly. He was singing, probably a song from the film they'd seen. When Rukmini saw Hiralal, she asked, with concern, "Did you eat, Ba?" Hiralal shook his head. "Why don't I heat the rice for you?" Moti shot one glance at his father, then went to his room, humming.

Rukmini lit the stove while Hiralal sat on the pirka. He remained silent as she heated the leftover rice and vegetables from the morning. Then, as she served him, she said, "I asked him not to drink, but he wouldn't listen."

Hiralal was eating.

"He even forced me to drink."

He tilted his head in surprise. "You drank?"

"Just a little," she said. "One glass of beer."

"Let's smell?" he said. He moved close to her face, and she opened her mouth and said, "Haaa," revealing her pink tongue. The smell of beer was negligible, but Hiralal felt his chest tighten. "You shouldn't have drunk."

"What could I do?" she said. "This is the first time he's spoken to me."

"Still," he said. He shook his head. His teeth clamped down on something hard, sending a shiver through his body. He extracted a small stone from his mouth and showed it to her. "The rice wasn't cleaned."

She took it from his hand. "I cleaned it thoroughly this morning."

"Well, you need to do it properly." He pushed the plate aside and said, "You must be more responsible. I thought you'd get him in line."

Her eyes filled with tears. "Just today he spoke—"

"I know," he said. "Don't drink with him from now on. Make him stop."

Later that night he regretted having spoken to her so harshly. She was a good girl, and Moti was starting to take an interest in her. Hiralal listened to the sounds from the couple's room. They were making love; Hiralal could hear Rukmini's soft sighs.

Once Chaudhari saheb got better, Hiralal could no longer go home in the afternoon. Besides, Moti stayed in his room all day and drank. By the time Hiralal got home in the evening, the house smelled like the bhatti from which Hiralal had once dragged Moti. The three ate together in the kitchen, and Moti couldn't keep his drunken eyes off Rukmini. Hiralal marveled at this change in his son. How did she do it? Hiralal watched her carefully. She had an earnest, childlike face, yet her eyes suddenly looked wise, as if they could sway the events of the world by merely gazing at them. Hiralal was startled.

In the mornings, while Moti was sleeping off his drunken stupor, Rukmini served food to Hiralal. One morning, she said, out of the blue, "At least now he's drinking at home." When Hiralal didn't respond, she said, "Ba, I'm trying."

"I'm not criticizing you."

That evening, Moti announced during dinner that he'd found a job as an office boy at a travel agency. He said this to Rukmini, although it was clear that she already knew and that the message was intended for Hiralal. "I'm starting tomorrow," he said, his eyes on his wife.

"That's very good," Hiralal said, trying not to show his surprise.

The next afternoon Hiralal went to Chaudhari saheb, who was studying some papers in his living room, and said, "Hujoor, do we have to go to the factory today?"

Without raising his eyes, Chaudhari saheb said, "No. Why?"

"I was wondering whether I could take the car. My daughter-in-law is ill; she needs to go to the hospital."

Now Chaudhari saheb looked up. "Go ahead. I have to prepare for a meeting with the managers tomorrow. Just make sure the car is here this evening."

His heart beating rapidly, Hiralal drove out of Chaudhari saheb's compound. He had never before lied to his boss.

When he got home, he expected to find Rukmini in the courtyard, but she wasn't there. The door to the house was locked from the outside, so he unlocked it, went upstairs, and softly called her name. Standing in the kitchen, wondering what to do next, he heard her come up the stairs. "Where have you been?" he asked, unable to hide his irritation.

"I just went to the neighbor's house," she said and started to fill the kettle.

He stopped her. "No, we're going out."

"Where?"

"I don't know where. I have the car."

She stood still, her eyes on him, and said, "Okay. I'll get dressed."

He watched as she limped to her room.

When she emerged, she was wearing a green sari with red seams. She hadn't put on any makeup. As they left the house, Hiralal saw a neighbor watching from her window.

"Where are we going?" Rukmini asked again once they were in the car.

He turned to her and smiled. "You tell me. It's your day. I borrowed the car especially for you."

"Really?" She appeared pleased. "But we'll have to come back soon so that I can cook dinner. It's Moti's first day at work, so I'm cooking goat."

"We'll be back in time," he said.

Because she couldn't name a place she wanted to visit, they drove around the city. They passed through New Road, with its bright shops and newspaper vendors. They circled the Tundikhel field, drove past Dharahara, its tower soaring up to the sky. She laughed at the heads of goats and pigs, their teeth bared, outside the Muslim butcher shops. "They look as if they're grinning," she said.

He smiled at her and said, "They're happy they don't have to think anymore."

She laughed.

Hiralal turned the car and headed south. "I know where we can go," he said at the traffic circle in Tripureswar, and sped toward Teku, then on to Tahachal. He drove quickly, passing small lorries, even taxis. Drivers honked at him, annoyed. He could sense that she was holding her breath, and he drove even faster, until she said, "Do you have to go this fast?"

He slowed down immediately, but by this time they were already in the outskirts of the city, in Swayambhu.

He parked the car at the bottom of the hill.

"Are we walking up?" she asked, calculating the hundreds of stairs leading to the stupa.

In his excitement he had forgotten about her limp. "We don't have to," he said. "We can circle the bottom in the car."

She squinted at the stupa. "No, we're already here. May as well go."

She took twice as long as he did to mount each step. Halfway up the staircase, she nearly fell, and he grabbed her arm. From then on, she leaned on him as they climbed. Monkeys roamed around them, chattering. One monkey held a baby monkey in her arm and monitored them cautiously. A large monkey chased smaller ones, who scattered, making frightened noises.

By the time the two reached the top, sweat was trickling down her forehead. She rested briefly before the large stupa and wiped her face with a small red handkerchief she'd pulled from her purse. They circled the stupa, then stood at the lookout.

"Moti liked to come here when he was a child," Hiralal said. She said nothing.

"He was like a monkey," Hiralal said and laughed. "So much energy."

"Tell me," she said, "what was your wife like?"

He was surprised at her boldness, the way she called her dead mother-in-law "your wife," as if Hiralal were a friend, not her father-in-law.

"She was like you," he said.

A haze hung in the air below them. "How was she like me?" She moved closer to him, and their shoulders touched.

Hiralal hoped no one he knew was in the temple. He wanted to say, She combed her hair just the way you do. But he knew he shouldn't. "I don't know," he said. "When I look at you —"

She took his hands in hers. "Do you miss her?"

He nodded. She played with his fingernails.

"What do you want me to do?" she asked.

"What do you mean? I don't want you to do anything."

"No, you want something from me. What is it?"

"I want you to take care of Moti. Make him stop drinking. Make him a responsible man. Give me grandchildren."

"No, that's not it," she said, shaking her head slowly. "That I'll do. But you want something else."

He realized that his knees were shaking, and so were his hands. "I don't know," he mumbled.

"I know what you want," she said. "But you have to promise me. Once you get it, you can't ask anything more of me."

Without fully understanding what he was agreeing to, he nodded, his heart pounding.

They walked down the steps in silence. Inside the car, she told him to drive behind the temple area. After they crossed Ring Road, which circled the city, she asked him to stop at an area off the road, in a clearing among trees that blocked their view of the surrounding houses.

She placed her hand on his chest and started rubbing, and he touched her shoulders and moved his face close to hers. As he kissed her, he felt like crying. She fumbled with his trousers, took his penis in her hand, and caressed it. He felt it rise and knew he should stop this, but something inside him had been released. "Why are you crying?" she asked. "Do you want to do this?" He didn't answer, but he wasn't surprised when he went limp in her hands. "You're getting small," she said, and he rested his head on her chest.

They drove back in silence, slowly, as the evening rush hour filled the streets with trucks, cars, three-wheelers, and mopeds. She was silent throughout the ride, and by the time he dropped her off at home, a slow burning had started in his stomach.

In Jawalakhel, Chaudhari saheb was still in the living room with his papers. "What did the doctors say?" he asked.

"Everything is all right," Hiralal said. "She just has the flu."

"Yes, everyone seems to be catching it these days."

After Hiralal got off the bus at Ratna Park and was walking through Indra Chowk, negotiating his way through the crowded marketplace, the noise around him turned distant, and his stomach began to convulse. Dizzy, he leaned against a pole.

At home, a strong smell of goat meat came from the kitchen. He went directly to his room and shut the door. The burning had now moved up to his chest and down to his hips and legs. Sweating, Hiralal took off his shirt and trousers and lay, face down, on the rug. He rested like this, his skin on fire. Only after about half an hour did the heat leave his body, and he got up and put on his clothes. Again, he looked at Rammaya's picture, and a tremendous wave of shame washed over his body. "Rammaya," he whispered, but couldn't bear to see her face. He took the picture off the wall and slipped it under his bed. Then he sat by the window. The sun had already gone down, and soon he saw Rudra walking by, twirling his shop keys on his finger. Rudra shouted, "I hear Moti has found a job."

"Yes," Hiralal said.

"Didn't I tell you?" Rudra said. "Amazing what a wife can do."

"Yes, you were right, Rudra."

"Soon you'll have grandchildren to look after." Rudra laughed, waved a hand, and walked on.

After Moti came home, Rukmini called Hiralal to dinner. "I'm not hungry," he said loudly. She knocked on his door, and when he opened it, she said softly, "You must eat something."

He shook his head, and turned his back to her as she whispered, "You must get hold of yourself."

He went to sit on his bed, and she followed him. "I thought you understood."

He was conscious that Moti was in the next room and that the door was open. "I can't live in this house with you anymore," he said quietly.

"What are you going to do? Where would you go?"

He had no answers. All he knew was that sooner or later Moti would sense what had happened between his wife and his father that afternoon.

"Don't you see?" she said. "It was bound to happen." She left the room.

He didn't join them for dinner, and later that night, when the sounds of their love-making filtered through his wall, he walked out of the house. He wandered for a long time, even after most of the shopkeepers had pulled down their shutters and turned off their lights. He moved through alleys and streets he'd never known existed. In Naxal, a mob of drunken young men followed him, challenging him to a fight. Hiralal merely quickened his steps.

He went home only when his legs were aching. Although he tiptoed up the stairs, Rukmini must have been awake. She opened her door and stepped out. "Where have you been?" she whispered angrily.

"Walking," Hiralal said.

"Don't you understand? What happened this afternoon—it was bound to happen. There was nothing you or I could do."

"No, I don't understand," he said. As he gazed at her under the weak lamp, his mind was quick with thoughts.

"Put her picture on the wall again," she said. She went into her room and shut the door.

He moved on to his room and reached under his bed for Rammaya's photograph. Her eyes were the same as when she smiled at their son or looked up at him when combing her hair in the courtyard. As if she were right behind him, he could smell the coconut in her hair, could smell her dhoti, with its faint aroma of onions and goat meat. "It was bound to happen," Rukmini had said. Hiralal held his wife's photograph and lay down. "What have you done, Rammaya?" he whispered. He closed his eyes, and felt as if he were floating, suspended in the air.

During the Festival

Gᴀɴᴇѕʜ lay on his back in bed, one hand behind his head, his legs dangling off the side, while his wife rummaged through the dresser for the sari to wear that evening. He watched her plump body in petticoat and bra, her fingers lingering on one sari, then another, finally pulling out one of red chiffon. When she turned and saw him watching her, she asked, "What's the matter? You don't want me to go?"

"No. You go," he said.

She asked him to help button her blouse, so he went over to her half-naked body, his heart hammering in his throat.

He went down to see her off through the courtyard, and climbed the stairs back to their apartment. He could imagine her walking down the street, her neatly combed hair pulled back, a tika on her forehead. He could imagine the taxi driver peeking at her in the rearview mirror, unable to take his eyes off her faintly powdered face, wondering what kind of a husband she went home to, how it would feel to lie next to her and hear her sigh under his caress. Ganesh could see her entering the wedding tent, adjusting her sari, her eyes appraising the crowd, familiar faces lighting up when they spotted her, a childhood friend of hers coming to greet her proprietarily, introducing her to guests, the men eyeing her from behind their wives.

He opened the door to the small balcony and stepped out. Four stories below, in the courtyard, two boys were playing marbles. In the opposite house, the new tenant, a young, bald man, leaned against the window, surveying the courtyard. When their eyes met, the bald man smiled. Ganesh didn't like him; he was too friendly, suspiciously friendly. So Ganesh barely nodded. The boys' arguments echoed amidst the frantic cries of the evening birds. The setting sun cast a saffron glow on the houses surrounding the courtyard. The evening, though beautiful, seemed alien to him.

He had recently told a friend at work that he did not understand his wife. He had said it casually, as if it were a joke. His friend blew into his cupped palms, as he always did when considering a serious matter. "Do you think your wife has a secret life?" he asked.

"There's something about her," Ganesh said, shaking his head. Lately he had been studying her; he watched her while she slept, tried to imagine her thoughts when she stirred eggplant or beans in the kitchen. He also wanted to know what she thought about when he wasn't around, what areas her mind lingered on. He suspected that her thoughts excluded him, and this possibility filled him with dismay, with pain.

They'd been married for three years, and Ganesh had not worried this way the first two years. Before he married, he lived on the second floor of a small house in Chhetrapati with his mother. Ganesh barely remembered his father, who died of a brain disease that no doctor or shaman had been able to cure. And there were rumors that Ganesh was really not his father's son; that he was the son of the man who had been his mother's lover for many years. It was his mother who had arranged

Ganesh's marriage. She'd sung the praises of his future bride—
"She has the most beautiful eyes"; "She's known in the neighborhood for her faultless manners"—until he too began to
think she would make a wonderful wife, even though he'd not
yet met her. When she first came into the house, he had been
surprised by her beauty. He'd seen pictures of her, but in person
she was ten times more striking. Her jet-black hair made a
lovely contrast with her fair complexion, and she had a long,
slim nose from which a diamond glinted whenever she smiled.
A mere glance from her made his heart beat rapidly, and when
she laughed, the tiny gap between her two front teeth made her
irresistibly charming. "Your daughter-in-law's face glows like
the sun," he heard relatives tell his mother, and everywhere he
and his new bride went, people commented on how his wife's
beauty would usher in good luck for the rest of their lives. He
had basked in the warmth of these comments, but later, that
pleasure had given way to wariness, for he couldn't believe that
such beauty could be enjoyed at no cost.

He tried to recall the exact moment when he first had doubts
about her; it was, he thought, when they were at the eastern
wall of the temple complex of Lord Pashupatinath on a sunny
day, looking down at the dirty Bagmati River. A young man
standing near them said to Ganesh's wife, "Look how filthy the
river is. Look there"—he pointed to a couple of women washing themselves contentedly, letting their soap suds drift into the
blackened water—"how uncivilized these people are. Look
there"—he gestured to a mass of garbage on the river's edge—
"our holy Bagmati River."

The man laughed, and Ganesh's wife laughed too, with an
abandon that Ganesh had found disconcerting.

"No one is doing anything about it," she'd told the young
man. "The politicians are more interested in their fat wives."

And then her laughter seemed to ring throughout the temple complex, mixing with the bells, reverberating with the chants of the priests. When they left the temple, Ganesh asked her, "Do you know that man?" And she said no. As they walked home that day, he compared his body with hers, and decided that he was a tight man, with muscles that were closed, restricting. He realized that he hardly moved his arms when he walked, whereas she constantly swirled her arms, sometimes scratching an itch on her face, at other times playing with her sari. Suddenly a phrase that had plagued his childhood echoed in his mind: "Mama's boy." That's what his friends called him whenever they saw him cling to his mother, his fist clutching the end of her sari. "The boy needs a father," he'd heard his relatives whisper among themselves. "Mama's boy," they'd called him, although they did so with affection. That day, walking away from the Pashupatinath Temple with his wife, he wondered whether his muscles were so constricted, and his body so closed, because he'd watched the world for so long from behind his mother's sari.

On his way home from work the next evening, he saw women in brilliant saris walking with their husbands, strolling down the street or rushing to keep appointments. It was the time of Indra Jatra festival, the eight-day festival in honor of Lord Indra, the ruler of heaven. Eons ago, Lord Indra had come down to the valley in disguise to steal scented white parijat flowers for his mother's annual fasting ritual. The powerful god was apprehended by the people of the Kathmandu Valley, bound with rope, and thrown in jail. Only after Indra's mother descended from heaven in search of her missing son did the valley inhabitants realize what they had done. As an apology, they initiated a great festival in his honor. They donned masks and danced, acted out folk dramas, and marched in celebratory processions. Everywhere around him, Ganesh saw people's faces filled with joy and excitement. He knew he should have enjoyed that excitement; instead, he felt as if a giant bird had descended from the sky and spread a shadow over the city.

Ganesh was in bed by the time his wife came home, and her cool skin startled him. Her petticoat brushed against him, her perfume wafted around him. Humming a tune, she played with his hair. After her breathing slowed, he slid out of bed and quietly went downstairs.

In the kitchen he turned on the lights, opened the cupboard, and poured himself a shot of the strong local liquor. The drink burned his throat. Under his breath he sang the song she had been humming. The warmth of the liquor spread to his thighs. He put on his coat and trudged down the stairs to the street. The knowledge that she was upstairs, unaware of his absence, filled him with excitement. The cloudless sky, the cold, shimmering stars, granted him a strange freedom, an expansion that came to him as a release in his lungs.

Just as he was walking beneath the clock tower in the city's center, it began to chime. Looking up, he discovered that it was three o'clock in the morning.

He climbed over the fence surrounding the Queen's Pond, took off his clothes, and dived in, not caring whether a police squad would approach. The chill of water invigorated him as he waded through the lilies floating on top. He wondered how long it would take, if he allowed himself to sink, for the water to fill his lungs. He thought of monsters with long tentacles that supposedly lived at the bottom, and he imagined them tearing into his flesh. Would his wife be able to recognize his body?

He heard the clock tower ring out four times, and he swam to the edge. When he reached his house and slipped under the bed covers, she murmured but didn't wake up.

Sunlight assailed his eyes when he woke the next morning. The late-morning heat on his bed had made him sweat, and his pajamas were sticking to the hairs on his chest. He reached for his cigarettes and lit one, propped up a pillow, and leaned against it. The light of day made last night's swim seem almost unreal.

When he turned the latch to the balcony door, he heard a steady *thump-thump-thump*. His wife was down in the courtyard, near the tap, beating a bundle of clothes against the cement slab. A few women stood close to her, talking, waiting to fill their pitchers. A small girl, her thumb in her mouth, watched his wife's movements while clinging to her mother, a widow who lived in the house opposite. He suddenly imagined climbing over the railing and letting himself fall down the four stories, his clothes swirling upward as the air pressed against them, the sensation of dropping underneath a clear, well-lit sky, the little girl spotting him in midair and excitedly reaching for her mother, her mother slowly turning her head, and, finally, *splat*, his consciousness fading, his wife's horror as the tap water steadily gushed into a brass pitcher.

Now his wife looked up and, seeing him lean against the railing, shouted, "The railing is weak!" He moved back a step and noticed the bald man across the courtyard watching them, the muscles on his arms protruding as his elbows rested on the window bar. The man smiled and nodded.

Ganesh quickly left the balcony.

He went to the cupboard and found a large black-and-white framed picture of their wedding, his wife looking directly at the camera, as if trying to stare it down. He looked happy; his head was tilted to one side, the beginning of a smile on his lips. It occurred to him that she may not have been happy on their wedding day; perhaps she had secretly wanted to marry another man, someone with more money, better looks, a prestigious family.

As he set the wedding picture back in the cupboard, his fingers brushed against another picture, one of his mother. He took it out. She was standing on the footsteps of a temple, which he recognized as Boudhha, the city's Buddhist temple, where hundreds of pilgrims congregated each day. It was an old photograph, probably taken right after he was born; the paper had yellowed at the corners. His mother was looking directly at the camera, the same way his wife had done. Maybe that's what women do, he thought. The photograph of his mother reminded him of people in the neighborhood whispering, when Ganesh was young, that he was the child of her union with her lover, not with his father. Throughout his childhood he had been haunted by an image of this so-called lover: a thin man with stick-like arms, sad eyes, and an aloof manner. One day when he was seven, he'd asked his mother whether she knew a tall man with sad eyes, and she had, with curiosity, scanned his face, then ruffled his hair and said no. He watched for such a man in his neighborhood and at the carnivals his mother took him to, carnivals with games and swings and giant wheels, but no one resembled the image that returned to him, again and again.

His wife cooked lunch, and while they ate, she brought up the wedding. "The tent was huge," she said. "It could have held a thousand guests, but there were only about a hundred. A woman was wearing a necklace with thirteen—no, twelve—big diamonds. Imagine wearing that! What a burden on your neck, and the fear you'd have while you wore it. A man there asked about you, said his office is down the hall from yours; he does the revenues or something like that."

She talked of the evening as though assured of his interest. Her words filled his mind so that his own thoughts clamored for room. In time, he grew angry and shifted his feet. "I'm not hungry," he said and walked out of the room and down the stairs.

His head throbbed with anger. She hadn't even asked what he'd done while she was away last evening. He felt humiliated. Outside, he took to the small road and alleys, with no direction in mind. He imagined going to his friend's house, standing beside the bed, where his friend would be reading a silly magazine, and declaring, "My wife is having an affair." Of course he didn't know whether that was true, but he wanted to reach the truth, no matter what it was, even through a lie.

The streets were crowded, and brightly dressed children chased one another through the throngs of people. In Durbar Square, Ganesh came upon a group of people playing drums and cymbals. A small boy, his face painted white, taunted a large man wearing a mask with wide, thick lips and large, glaring eyes. Peacock feathers rose from the back of his head, and frills on the seams of his vest flew in every direction as he waved his arms in circles. The little boy danced near the man and made faces at him. The masked man, also dancing, attempted to strike the boy—whether as an act or in real anger, it was hard to tell—at which point the music reached a crescendo and then resumed its normal beat. The masked man swooned with the powers of a deity, and the onlookers gave him wide berth.

Ganesh leaned against the side of a house and watched. People appeared at windows, and the crowd around the performers thickened. Every time the boy's darting figure came close to the masked man, the spectators let out a collective gasp, and drums threatened to crack the narrow sky above. And every time the boy approached the man, Ganesh clearly saw the boy's apprehension, the danger, the thrill of being so close to a deity whose slap could send him sprawling across the brick street. When the boy escaped punishment, however, Ganesh watched the masked dancer, saw his humiliation, the lack of appreciation from the crowd, the maddening fury of his not being able to silence the teaser.

At one point the masked man, his legs apart for a second's break in rhythm, threw a wild look right at Ganesh, who flattened himself against the wall like a shadow, a thrill running through his limbs.

She waited for him, circles under her eyes, at the front of the house and demanded to know why he'd walked out like that, where he'd gone. "Everything is all right," he said. "It's just that lately my heart's been restless." He went inside and lay on his bed.

She came and set a serving of dal-bhat on the side table, then put her hand on his chest, as if to calm his heart. "What's wrong?" she asked. "Is everything all right at work?"

He nodded and closed his eyes. Her hand on his chest felt good, but he feared that if he let it stay there, he would feel even weaker, so he got up and rubbed his eyes. "I'm hungry," he said and lifted the plate. He ate quickly, and realized only after he'd finished that she was not eating with him.

That night, after he was sure she was asleep, he draped a shawl around his back and moved to the balcony. The big moon hung above the courtyard. There was a light in the bald man's window, but the curtains were drawn. Ganesh could see a figure, fading and reappearing, and he sat on the cold floor of the balcony. The figure moved about the room, its silhouette becoming clear, then disappearing.

He awoke, just before dawn, with the chirping of birds, to discover that his feet were cold. Shivering, he went back to bed.

In the morning, she asked for some money so that she could go to the market. He reached into his pocket and quietly handed her a fifty-rupee note. She said, "But I also need to buy rice and kerosene." He pulled out another fifty-rupee note.

That evening, when he came home from work, the stove was empty, and she was nowhere to be found. There was a musty smell in their bedroom, as if someone else had been there. His body grew limp, and he sat on the bed.

Ganesh went to a bar with his friend. They squeezed themselves onto a bench in a corner, ordered rum and spicy minced buff, and talked of work, colleagues, the city, and food. The other conversations in the room buzzed like flies near their ears. Soon, Ganesh's head started to float.

"So, how is your wife?" the friend asked, chuckling.

"She has a lover," Ganesh said, attempting to be grave, but somehow laughter rose from his throat. His friend stared at him for a moment; then he, too, broke into a smile. They both fell into a fit, stamping their feet and spilling drinks on the table. And suddenly, as if the laughter had been a necessary prelude, Ganesh found himself crying. The customers stared in his direction, and the owner came over to ask whether he was all right.

Ganesh simply shook his head and repeated, "How could she do this?"

After he calmed down, he and his friend talked about the festival of Dashain, only a few weeks away, when they would slaughter goats as sacrifice to appease the Goddess Durga. "I wonder how many of them I can slaughter," Ganesh said. "The last time, I killed four before I had enough."

The friend called for more drinks.

"I can't drink anymore," Ganesh said. His stomach was burning, and the room had become hazy.

"Mama's boy," his friend said, laughing. "I thought you were stronger than this."

"Don't call me that."

"What? You're a mama's boy."

"Really?" he said. "You want to see how much I can drink?" He asked the owner to bring another jar of the local liquor, and he drank, his eyes on his friend, who was now having a hard time keeping up with him. "So, who's a mama's boy?" he said. "Huh? Tell me, bastard." His throat and his belly were on fire, but he kept drinking and needling his friend, who finally said, "All right, all right. I take it back."

The hours passed, and they were the only customers in the bar, so they staggered out, clapping each other's back and singing songs of friendship. The street lights shone on them, exposing their delirious faces. When they saw a wedding procession on the way home, they joined the crowd, dancing behind the band.

His wife didn't bring him tea the next morning, and Ganesh staggered to the window. There she was, in the courtyard, talking to the bald man, whose back was turned toward him. Ganesh waited, his head throbbing from last night's alcohol. The man laughed and his wife followed suit, covering her mouth with her hand. She called to one of the kids playing in the courtyard and pointed at the man, who shook his head vigorously and laughed again. Ganesh retreated. He went to the bedroom, where he found some aspirin, and swallowed them without water.

Later, when she came inside, he was lying on the bed, his

face toward the wall. She sang in the kitchen, and he listened, trying to detect a new tone, a foreign melody.

She appeared with a glass of tea. "Isn't it time to wake up now?" she asked him.

He glanced at his watch; it was nearly time to go to the office.

On the bus his mind kept replaying the courtyard scene, and with each repetition he felt tiny stabs in his stomach. He tried to tell himself that she had merely been talking to the man, but an aura of secrecy, of deceit, surrounded the scene, and he could picture them kissing on the bald man's bed, her fingers feeling his muscles.

At work his friend approached and said, "It was fun last night, eh? I haven't drunk like that in a long time, not since last year's festival." He paused. "What happened? Was your wife angry?"

Ganesh shrugged his shoulders.

"She'll be all right," the friend said. "By the time you get home."

That evening Ganesh went by the pond on the way home. He shivered; it was hard to believe that he actually dived into that dirty water the other night.

It was dark when he reached his house. Walking through the courtyard, he nearly bumped into someone. It was the bald man, his muscular arms shining in the light coming from one of the windows. Ganesh thought, He's going to kill me. The man's voice floated toward him in the dark: "I know your wife."

Ganesh couldn't see the man's face; it was half in shadow. "I saw you together," Ganesh eventually said. "Laughing." He walked up the stairs to his apartment.

His wife met him at the door. "Who was that man? Was he drunk?"

He answered, "Your lover."

"Don't joke. Who was he?"

"No joke," he said. "You should have told me."

She turned and walked to the kitchen, and he followed her. "How long has this been going on?" His breath was stuck high in his throat.

Her back to him, she began slicing tomatoes.

"It doesn't matter now," he said, his hands shaking. "I won't get angry. I won't shout at you. I'll let you do whatever you want. That way, I may get some peace."

She uttered a sharp "Aiya" and put her index finger in her mouth. He went to her, pried out the finger, and inspected it. The cut was small, right above the second joint. He fetched the rubbing alcohol and patted her wound. She didn't look at his face but watched the cut with growing dismay.

"Here. I'll slice the tomatoes," he said.

"You are jealous, suspicious. You think I have a lover?"

"I don't know," he said. "I really don't know." He waited for her to say something.

"Would you kill him if you thought he was my lover?"

"Who? The man downstairs?"

She seemed exasperated. "No, no," she said. "My lover, any lover." Something occurred to her. "Who was that man downstairs?"

He didn't answer her and finished cutting the tomatoes.

Dust rose inside the bus, tiny particles glittering in the afternoon sun. The bus lurched toward its destination, the temple of the Goddess Durga on the outskirts of the city. His wife was asleep, her head resting against the window. In front of them sat a man with four hens, their feet tied together. With every jolt, the hens tried to rise in the air, cackling insanely, sending feathers floating up and down the length of the bus. The kohl on his wife's eyelids trickled down her cheeks. Ganesh smiled and stretched his legs. He looked forward to the ceremony at the temple, where his relatives would ask him to kill goats because he was good at it. And Ganesh would hoist the khukri knife high in the air, its sharpened edge glinting in the dusk, amid the appreciative cries of the onlookers.

Another vision came to him. He was sitting in the middle of a field, his mother in her petticoat leaning over him, smiling and whispering. Blood was running down his nose, soaking the front of his shirt, trickling down his thighs and into the earth, where his friend was waiting with an open tongue. Then his wife leaped out of a photograph and shook her finger at him, and the dancing bald man had a face that looked much like his own. Everything grew silent, a bird cried—and he opened his eyes and looked around. The bus had stopped, caught in a traffic jam.

He was tired, as if he'd been walking for a long time. He woke up his wife.

"What?" she said, her eyes bleary, sweat like dew above her upper lip.

"I'm not sure," he said.

"About what?"

"Whether I can kill a goat today."

She searched his face. "What's the matter? You've never complained before."

The hens once again rose in the air and sprayed them with feathers.

"Look," he said. He lifted his hands. They were shaking.

She picked a feather from his head and ruffled his hair. Then she dabbed the sweat on his cheeks with the end of her sari. "You don't have to kill a goat if you don't want to."

Her hand on his face felt good. "But what will everyone say? They will laugh at me."

"Who cares?" she said. "What can it do to us?" His eyes

closed; he felt her lips brush against his cheek. "My mama's boy," she whispered. "My sweet, sweet mama's boy." Now her lips were nibbling at his ear, and he opened his eyes. The man with the hens was staring at them, and he felt embarrassed, but he didn't stop her; her words were soothing.

The bus came to a stop. They got out, clutching the bundles of rice and fruit they had brought to offer the gods. In front of them was a large field filled with cars and trucks, and, in the distance, the temple's pagoda.

As they joined the crowd moving toward the temple, some of Ganesh's fatigue vanished. He stopped to take off his shoes; the grass felt good beneath his feet. He shifted the bundle of rice he was carrying, and as they walked on, he touched his wife's hand with his free hand. She looked at his face quizzically, then took his hand in hers. The sky was bright blue, and the sun shone on their faces. The temple bells sounded, a clear *ding-dong* that reverberated inside his body, then expanded into their surroundings.

As the crowd around them chanted songs praising the Mother Goddess, he briefly thought of his wife's lover, but in this crowd, with its fervent devotion, the man had become inconsequential, faceless, dissolving into the crowd in which Ganesh was moving.

The Room Next Door

THE MAN had been squatting for hours on her front veranda, a besotted smile on his face as he squinted at the sun, but Mohandas, Aunt Shakuntala's husband, had not yet turned up. Aunt Shakuntala had told the man, "Come back some other time. My husband is not here." The man merely looked at her, smiled, and did not budge an inch. What kind of a husband was she married to, Aunt Shakuntala thought, who asks people to come, for whatever reason on earth, and vanishes for hours, leaving her with the burden of taking care of them, especially on a Saturday, when everyone else is relaxing? God knows she didn't have time for this.

Aunt Shakuntala had been raised by parents who doted on her, told her repeatedly that the man she'd marry would be the luckiest husband on earth. Yet here she was, stuck with Mohandas, who was not only indolent but didn't appreciate her. Hadn't she given him two fine children, a son and a daughter who were bright, hardworking, and obedient? Didn't she keep an immaculate house? Hadn't she gained tremendous respect from neighbors and relatives for the way she handled the household and the way she reared their children? To everyone, old and young alike, she was Aunt Shakuntala.

She brought the man a glass of tea. By this time, his head was in his hands, and he was dozing. "Here." She set down the glass. "You may as well drink this." He woke up. She hoped her tone had made it clear that catering to strangers was not exactly what she'd been born to do. The man smiled obsequiously, an ugly mole on his upper lip stretching with his mouth, and raised a hand in gratitude. She told him, "After drinking the tea, you leave." He beamed.

Mohandas was an irresponsible man. He was lazy, absent-minded, obstinate—an idiot. Yes, he is an idiot, repeated Aunt Shakuntala to herself. A few days ago, he brought home a sadhu, a Shiva devotee, whom he'd found wandering around, and put him up in the living room for a week. The sadhu, smelling of old clothes and ashes, lay sprawled on the sofa all day, stroking his long black beard. He asked Aunt Shakuntala for tea and sweets, and when she confronted Mohandas, all he said was: "The holy man has no place to live. What's the harm in giving him a roof for a while?" She replied that she wasn't born to cater to strangers, and he told her, "You need some compassion in your heart." Last year, when it was announced that three clerks in the government bank where Mohandas worked were to be promoted, he did not go to the local district officer, a distant cousin of hers, who could have exerted influence in the matter. He kept putting it off, making excuses like "Today I have a headache" or "I think he'll be very busy today." When the final announcement was made, and Mohandas wasn't one of those promoted, he merely commented, "Oh, well, my time will come," stretched, yawned, and went to the local tea shop to talk with the idlers who stayed there all day, smoking their cigarettes.

This man on the veranda had shown up at her house a few days ago, speaking very little but smiling profusely, and Mohandas had given him a few rupees. In answer to Aunt Shakuntala, Mohandas explained that the man came from a few towns over, that he was one of those fixed features of the street you find in every small town. His nickname was Lamfu, which meant *stupid,* a name someone had cruelly thrown at him in childhood because he showed signs of being retarded.

Lamfu was one of the numerous jobless men her husband befriended on the streets, invited to the house, and tried to find a job for, as if all he had to do was raise a finger and work would appear. His own job as a clerk in the government office did not carry prestige (it would have, Aunt Shakuntala thought, had he hustled to get that promotion), but his name, bestowed on him by his ancestors, did. The famous Bhandari Brahmins had owned land all over town only twenty years before, until the government decided to change the laws. Now they had only a tiny strip of land on the east side of town, where some farmers made their living. For Aunt Shakuntala, however, her husband's family name was one of his few virtues.

Mohandas was different when they'd first married, or that's how it seemed to her now. He had been hardworking and ambitious, and he'd listened to her advice. But gradually a change had come over him, like a disease. He mocked her words, her attitude, and told her that she was too controlling, that she cared too much about what society thought. By the third year of their marriage, after both the children were born, he had stopped talking to her softly in bed at night about the events of the day. He would read a book and then fell asleep, his back to her. It hurt her, this indifference, and she grew bitter. She took to sleeping in another room. Sometimes she did wonder whether something in her character had caused this change; she asked herself whether she tried too hard to control everything around her. But she believed that unless she did so, things would become worse, and Mohandas, who was casual about many aspects of life, would let their lives slide. As for caring too much about what society thought, Aunt Shakuntala reasoned that she lived among other people, not in an isolated world, the way Mohandas did, and in order to gain respect, she had to care about what relatives and neighbors thought of her.

The August afternoon, with its still air and heat, made Aunt Shakuntala lazy. This was the time for her daily nap, but with Lamfu sitting on her veranda, it was out of the question. And when Aunt Shakuntala didn't get her nap, she became irritable.

She took several deep breaths and decided she would wait for the mailman to see whether there were any letters from her children. Sanu and Shanti were attending separate colleges in Kathmandu city, which was a day's bus ride from the village, near Pokhara, where Aunt Shakuntala and Mohandas lived. Three weeks earlier, Aunt Shakuntala had received a letter from Sanu telling her about his seventeenth birthday, how he and his friends had gone to Bhrikuti Mandap amusement park, where they rode carousels and ate pistachio ice cream. It was the longest letter he'd written—a full two pages. Her daughter, Shanti, had not written for nearly two months. At night, Aunt Shakuntala lay awake, unable to sleep, worrying. When she did manage to sleep, she dreamed about ugly things happening to her daughter. Three nights ago, she dreamed that Shanti had fallen into a well and was shouting for help.

Lamfu had finished his tea and was dozing again, this time with his head against the wall and his mouth open. Aunt Shakuntala leaned in the doorway and watched him. He seemed not to have a care in the world. She envied the man, his lack of worries.

Someone passing by outside shouted, "Namaste, namaste." She opened the gate and recognized her neighbor, Mister Pandey, as he was called by everyone in the neighborhood, because he always wore suits and ties. He was a first-class officer at the Agricultural Development Bank. "Namaste, Mister Pandey," she said.

"All's well, Aunt Shakuntala?" he asked. "How is Mohandas-ji?"

"Who knows?" she said.

Mister Pandey chuckled and shook his head. "I just passed him at the tea shop." He seemed about to say something more but changed his mind. "And how are the children?"

She told him they were fine. After some more pleasantries, Mister Pandey left, and Aunt Shakuntala watched him go down the street. What a gentleman he was, and how quickly he had risen through the ranks in his office. He hobnobbed with all the powerful people in the area. For a brief moment Aunt Shakuntala wondered how her life would have been had she married Mister Pandey instead of Mohandas. The thought made her feel guilty, and she quickly dismissed it. Mohandas was her husband, and that was that.

The mailman, a thin man with whiskers, appeared, but he passed by, giving her an almost mournful look.

"Postman-ji," she said loudly, and Lamfu jerked his head up. "You haven't delivered any letters for five weeks."

The postman turned and said, in a sad voice, "If there were letters, I would have given them to you. What should I do, hajoor? Set up a letter-manufacturing company?" For a man with a sad face, she thought, he had a cruel manner.

Lamfu was studying her intently, as though trying to figure out what she was really like. She grew self-conscious and could not resist saying, loudly, "I told you, my husband is not here. Now leave!" She pointed toward the road.

Lamfu gave her a reproachful look and, placing his hands on his knees, stood. As he left, he said, "Tomorrow."

She went in and lay down on her bed, thinking of various

reasons for Shanti's not writing to her—she had flu; she was in the midst of her final exams—but an ominous feeling swept over her. It was unlike Shanti not to write. Ever since leaving for the capital, Shanti had written every two weeks. Her letters were full of details about her life in the bigger city, unlike Sanu's letters, which described the weather and his classes. It was as if Shanti relished those moments of writing to her mother about her friends, the restaurants in the city, the movies she had seen, and, sometimes, about a boy who had teased her or wanted to take her to a restaurant. Whenever Shanti wrote about boys, Aunt Shakuntala became anxious. She knew Kathmandu girls were modern and did not think twice about associating with many boys. Shanti was very pretty, with a long oval face and large eyes, and before she left for Kathmandu the neighborhood boys used to follow her on her way to school. What if Shanti had become involved with a big-city boy? Every time this thought occurred to her, Aunt Shakuntala had to calm herself. Her daughter had always spoken disparagingly of the boys who hung around her like fleas. And she revealed everything to her mother, didn't she?

Her husband came home that evening, whistling some religious tune and looked at her mockingly when he found her in bed. She had slept, she realized to her shame, for three and a half hours. She told him in anger, "Who do you think you are? Some kind of king, with servants at his disposal to take care of any lunatic you deem worthy of worship? What do you think this house is—made a home by my blood and sweat? A hotel where I am the cleaning woman?"

Her husband continued to regard her with half a smile. When she finished, he muttered under his breath, "Silly woman," and walked into the kitchen, looking for something to drink. Aunt Shakuntala fell back on the bed.

Later, she went to sit beside him on the veranda and watch the sunset. He was staring into the horizon and did not even acknowledge her presence. She pretended to ignore him for some time, adjusting her hair and prying out dirt from under her fingernails. When it seemed as though he was not going to pay her any attention, she cleared her throat and said, "The postman did not bring any letters today." She waited for his reaction, but when he said nothing, she added, "I haven't heard from Shanti for months."

"Don't exaggerate," he said, his voice barely audible.

"I think something has happened to her."

"Sanu would let us know if something had happened, wouldn't he? Now stop this nonsense."

She felt helpless, vulnerable. She needed to talk to him about the children. After all, he was their father.

"We should call Rabindra and ask him to check on her," she said. Rabindra, a distant relative, lived in Kathmandu and had agreed to keep an eye on Sanu and Shanti.

"Shakuntala, don't fret. Your children are grown up now. Don't treat them as if they're suckling babies."

"I am a mother," she said, a lump rising in her throat. "If I don't worry about my children, who will I worry about?" She hoped that her trembling voice would have some effect on him.

He continued to assess the sunset, but suddenly he said, "All right. I will talk to Rabindra." Then, in a voice that was almost tender, he added, "You worry too much."

She discovered, three days after her husband talked to Rabindra, what was wrong.

Early in the morning, the daughter of their neighbor Ram Charan came to get Mohandas. Somebody from Kathmandu was on the phone for him at her father's house, the only one in the area with a telephone. Right then, Aunt Shakuntala knew that something terrible had happened. She woke Mohandas, who hurriedly put on his trousers and ran to Ram Charan's house. Aunt Shakuntala waited on the veranda, pacing, praying that he'd come back to tell her that everything was all right. When Mohandas did return, after what seemed like hours, he stood in front of her, hesitating, and then said that Shanti was pregnant. By some boy at the college, whose whereabouts were now unknown. Shanti had broken down in front of Rabindra in her small room in the dormitory. She was already in her fourth month. She had stopped writing home because she was scared. She did not know, she had said, that doing it once could make her pregnant. The boy had promised to marry her, but he'd gone away.

Aunt Shakuntala's knees felt weak, and she sat down on the cold veranda. Had the neighbor, Ram Charan, heard the conversation? she wanted to ask, but the words became stuck in her throat. The sun had moved up the horizon, and in the distance a truck rumbled on the highway. Mohandas stood beside her, his hand on the railing. She wished she could go back to bed and wake up a different person.

An hour later, Mohandas left for Kathmandu to bring Shanti home.

Aunt Shakuntala stayed on the veranda, watching school-children with their heavy backpacks walk past the house. What was to be done now? They would have to make sure that no one, not a single soul outside the family, learned about Shanti's condition. The thought of her daughter's figure swollen and deformed brought the taste of vomit to Aunt Shakuntala's throat. Of course the baby would have to go; there was no question about that. They would find an orphanage. She certainly did not expect any resistance from her daughter, but if Shanti wanted to keep the baby, Aunt Shakuntala would give her such a thorough beating that the girl would never mention it again.

During the next two days, Aunt Shakuntala kept to herself. When Ram Charan came to inquire if everything was all right, she told him that Shanti was having some health problems and Mohandas had gone to fetch her. On the streets, she avoided people's eyes, her shame causing her to assume that people knew the secret.

Lamfu came by every morning, even though Aunt Shakuntala had told him that Mohandas had left town. It was as if Lamfu hadn't heard; he seemed content to just sit on the veranda. Every two hours or so he would smoke a bidi, and the pungent smell would drift into the bedroom and sting Aunt Shakuntala's nostrils. She would tell him to stop, and he'd obliged, smiling as he put out the bidi. Then he would lie against the wall and doze. There was something so innocent about his face, his being so oblivious of what people thought of him, that Aunt Shakuntala was envious. She gave him tea every morning, and he drank it eagerly, with loud smacking noises. The gratitude on his face touched her, and once or twice she even offered him slices of bread.

The afternoon before her husband was to return, Nandini, Aunt Shakuntala's niece who lived down the road, came for a visit. She was a thin woman with dark circles under her pleading, sunken eyes.

"Where's Mohandas, Mama?" Nandini asked after slowly looking around the house. She had a penchant for family drama, and Aunt Shakuntala was apprehensive.

"Oh, he has gone to Kathmandu," she said. "How's the baby?"

"He was coughing all night. I took him to the doctor, but he's not any better."

In the kitchen, Nandini helped herself to an orange Aunt Shakuntala had been saving for herself and then asked, "Have you gotten a letter from Shanti yet?"

Aunt Shakuntala had forgotten that she'd told Nandini, in a moment of frustration, that Shanti had not written lately. "Yes," she said.

"There must be many boys at her college," Nandini said, concentrating on the orange. Aunt Shakuntala knew Nandini was baiting her.

"She spends all her time with her books," Aunt Shakuntala said casually as she poured water in the kettle for tea. "She wants to be an engineer."

Nandini came close to her and whispered, "Did you hear about Jayaram's daughter Bijaya?"

Aunt Shakuntala shook her head.

Nandini looked left and right and said in a low voice, "They took her to India to get rid of the baby."

"I didn't know she was pregnant," Aunt Shakuntala said, a cold fear clenching her stomach.

"Oh, yes, everyone knows. It was a bus driver. You know how that Bijaya was, sashaying her hips for every low-life in town. I used to tell her mother: Watch your daughter. Now I say they deserve it. But to kill the bastard baby? *Chee, chee.* Whole family name down the drain. Who'd marry her now?"

Nandini continued with the town gossip until Aunt Shakuntala feigned a headache.

That evening she sat in the kitchen, watching the water from the white rice run down the side of the pot on the stove. She thought about her dreams for her children, how they would grow and become educated and establish names for themselves. They were not like her, she acknowledged. They knew so much, much more than she did at their age. Now Shanti had crushed her dreams.

Her husband came home early the next morning, with Shanti at his side.

Aunt Shakuntala forced herself to look at her daughter, her belly. There seemed to be a slight protrusion, but it was hard to tell, because Shanti was wearing a white shawl. Soon, she would start to show. The skin above Shanti's eyes was chapped, and her lips had a bluish tinge. Her eyes were pale and sunken, almost like Nandini's.

Shanti stayed by the door, as if she were a new servant. Aunt Shakuntala turned to face the window, not knowing what words would come out of her mouth should she attempt to speak.

"Come, no use standing there," Mohandas said to Shanti, not unkindly. "Go to your room." And the daughter, swathed in shame, made her way to the room she and her mother used to share. With that single act, she left no choice for her mother but to sleep in her husband's bed, the man she had not slept with for years.

In bed that night, Mohandas's figure, tall and angular, lay so close to Aunt Shakuntala that she felt strange. While she knew his mind inside out, his body was unfamiliar to her.

After he fell asleep, Aunt Shakuntala set her feet down on the cold floor and walked to the next room. Through the door, halfway open, she saw that her daughter was not sleeping. Barely visible in the dark, she was sitting on the bed, her head between her knees, which were pulled up tight. Sensing someone's presence at the door, Shanti looked up, her eyes wide and dry.

Her daughter's eyes reminded Aunt Shakuntala of a frightened animal's. She went back to her room.

The next morning she woke earlier than usual and bathed

beside the well in the backyard. Her neighbor from the adjacent house greeted her. "Such a nice morning, isn't it, Aunt Shakuntala. Such clear skies and sharp air." Aunt Shakuntala did not share the enthusiasm; she had hardly slept last night.

After her bath, she went to the prayer room and conducted puja half-heartedly. Even the statue of Lord Ganesh, with his long elephant trunk, appeared dull and lethargic today. Shanti was awake; Aunt Shakuntala had peeked into the room before going to the backyard. She heard Mohandas whistling in his room, and she went to him without completing the puja ceremony.

"We'll have to make preparations," she said, as he put on his trousers. Seeing her husband get dressed was a rare sight these days.

"Preparations?" he asked.

"For Shanti," she whispered. "She should not go out. The neighbors should not see."

"Oh." Mohandas looked thoughtful for a moment but then started whistling again.

"We will have to get a midwife from another town," she said.

He stopped whistling. "Do you think it will be a boy or a girl?"

"What does it matter? It won't stay with us," she said, slamming the door shut so that Shanti wouldn't hear.

"It won't?" Mohandas said, combing his hair.

"Do you know what you're saying?"

"I am not saying anything," he said calmly, ignoring the rise in her voice. He pointed toward Shanti's room. "What is *she* saying?"

Aunt Shakuntala went to the kitchen, where, as she prepared the morning meal, she made no attempt to quiet the banging of the dishes.

★

As the weeks turned into months, Aunt Shakuntala forbade Shanti to step out of the house. Shanti responded by sulking, but, to Aunt Shakuntala's surprise, she complied.

"You can't hide it," Mohandas told Aunt Shakuntala. "What's the use?"

Sometimes Aunt Shakuntala found Shanti standing in the kitchen, her hands resting on her belly, a faraway smile on her lips.

Nandini came sniffing about, as usual. "Where's my young sister? How's her health?" But Aunt Shakuntala wouldn't let her see Shanti, who, she made sure, remained in her room when anyone came to the house.

"Is something wrong?" Nandini asked, her eyes filled with mock concern. "I've been hearing things."

"What things?" Aunt Shakuntala said, hands on her hips.

"Oh, this and that," Nandini said vaguely and sighed. "You know how people talk." She was about to say more when Aunt Shakuntala interrupted. "I have work to do," she said and went out to the garden to pull some weeds.

A few weeks later, Ram Charan's wife came to the door and said, "How come I haven't seen Shanti around? Is she ill?"

"Yes, she's very ill," Aunt Shakuntala said and didn't let her in the house.

Whenever Aunt Shakuntala walked through the neighborhood, she felt that people on balconies and at windows were watching her, laughing.

"People know," she told Mohandas at night.

"I told you," Mohandas said. "You can't hide such a thing. What's done is done. You may as well accept it."

As she watched her husband sleep soundly that night, she had the urge to kick him on the back, to shout, "Do something, for God's sake!"

On her next visit, Nandini said, with a hurt expression,

"Everyone knows, Auntie. At least you could have told me. I am family." Then, without Aunt Shakuntala's permission, she barged into Shanti's room. Shanti was sitting on the chair, staring at the wall, her stomach swollen. Nandini said, "How are you, bahini?" And Shanti turned her head away.

"What month?" Nandini asked Aunt Shakuntala.

"Eighth."

Nandini's lips twitched. "We'll have to make preparations."

Aunt Shakuntala pushed her out of the room, shut Shanti's door, and said, "Everyone knows? How?"

"People suspect, Auntie. They've been asking me."

"What did you tell them?"

"What do you think I told them?" Nandini said with a look of martyrdom. "I said it was all nonsense."

One frosty morning Shanti went into labor. Lying in bed, she writhed in pain and clamped her teeth on a towel. Aunt Shakuntala sent Lamfu to fetch the midwife. The man had become a permanent fixture on the veranda by now, smoking his bidi and slurping his tea.

The baby was born, a big, dark boy with a mark on his left cheek. Without touching him, Aunt Shakuntala ordered the midwife to take him to the next room before his mother could see him. Then she gave the old woman an extra fifteen rupees and demanded that she not tell anyone of the delivery. After the midwife left, Aunt Shakuntala sat on the veranda. Although it was cold, she could feel sweat in her armpits. She didn't want to get up, but the baby had to be fed.

In the kitchen, Aunt Shakuntala warmed some milk and poured it into a plastic nursing bottle she'd secretly purchased a few days ago. She went to her room and stood beside him as he lay swaddled in old clothes. It was hard to say whether the newborn was ugly or beautiful. He was dark, which led Aunt Shakuntala to wonder whether his father was a madhisey from the flatlands down south. As she looked closer, however, the baby appeared charming, with large brown eyes and long eyelashes and dimples in his cheeks. It perplexed her that she had the absurd desire to define his beauty. It did not matter, she had to remind herself. He was going to go to an orphanage. She picked up the baby and, holding him in her arms, inserted the bottle nipple into his mouth. The baby sucked rapidly, his eyes shut tight.

That afternoon, when she was taking tea to Lamfu, she found him peering inside the door.

"What do you want?" she asked.

"Beautiful, beautiful," the man said, pointing toward the room where the baby was sleeping.

"No," she said.

"Beautiful, beautiful," he said again, shaking his head in admiration. "Lord Krishna," he said, taking the glass of tea. Aunt Shakuntala looked at him in distaste. He did not know what a calamity the child had brought to the house. Lord Krishna! No one should speak of the Lord in vain!

When she went to Shanti's room, she found her awake, her face as pale as a bedsheet. The girl looked pleadingly at her mother. Aunt Shakuntala had told Mohandas that she would not let Shanti see the baby, but now, at the sight of her daughter's face, she thought, Well, the baby isn't going to remain in the house much longer. Let her see the baby; let her see the shame she has brought on this home. She picked up the baby from the other room and brought him to his mother. Shanti held the child in her arms, and, after gazing into his eyes and running her finger across his face, burst into tears. Aunt Shakuntala snatched the child away and took him to her room, where, after holding him at arm's length and inspecting him, she was once again filled with the curious desire to define his beauty. She and the baby stared at each other for a long time. Reaching out with a finger to touch his lips, she realized what she was doing and drew back. She wanted the baby whisked away as soon as possible, before any of the neighbors visited.

When Mohandas came home that evening, she pulled him out to the veranda so that Shanti could not hear them.

"I don't know, woman," he said, after listening to her tirade about the urgency of sending the baby to an orphanage.

"What do you not know?"

"It is her child, after all."

"Her child? Have you lost your mind? What will the neighbors say when they see that baby running around the street? Will they think he's from the same Bhandari family that ruled this town?"

"You are foolish," her husband said in a matter-of-fact tone.

They heard sobbing noises, and Aunt Shakuntala rushed back inside. Shanti was holding the child tightly in her arms.

"I will not let him go," Shanti said. "You just try."

"This matter is not for discussion," her mother replied.

Mohandas appeared behind her. "Maybe we need to find Shanti a husband."

"Who do you think will marry her, you imbecile?" Aunt Shakuntala said.

"Him," said her husband, pointing toward the veranda and Lamfu, his cheeks sagging in the evening light, his teeth yellow and stained from years of smoking bidi.

Now that Shanti had smelled and touched her son, she threatened to leave the house if he were sent to an orphanage.

Aunt Shakuntala had challenged her daughter: "Go, go, leave. We'll see how long you survive in that world out there, carrying the shame hidden underneath your shawl." But when Shanti started to bundle up her clothes in a small plastic bag, Aunt Shakuntala gripped her daughter's arm, forbidding her to leave.

Shanti said, in a cold voice, "Mother, my baby's presence only brings you shame, so it is best for both of us to leave."

Mohandas stayed to the side, not offering any assistance, leaning his angular body against the wall, a half-smile on his face.

No matter how hard she tried, Aunt Shakuntala, a mother, could not let Shanti go out into the world to depend upon other people's mercy. Taking care of that bastard baby would eat away at Shanti, she knew. The baby was cursed and would suck the blood of those who fed him.

So she yielded. She gave Shanti the nursing bottle filled with warm milk and said, "Here, I'll say nothing more in this house. You do whatever you want."

When Shanti learned that she was to marry Lamfu, she did not protest, although a shadow lingered on her face. Yet she seemed determined to keep the child at any cost.

So it happened. Shanti was married to Lamfu. It was a small ceremony, but to Aunt Shakuntala the four hours seemed to stretch for days.

The priest chanted mantras and threw rice on the pyre, his bald head bobbing up and down to the rhythm of the Sanskrit chants. Aunt Shakuntala looked at her soon-to-be son-in-law. She was sure that Lamfu, with his idiotic smile and half a brain, barely understood what was happening in his life.

After the ceremony, the guests flocked to the buffet table on the lawn. They attacked the rice pilaf, chicken and goat curry, and steaming containers of spinach and cauliflower. They heaped their plates and talked with their mouths full. These people, thought Aunt Shakuntala; they will gorge themselves on our food and talk behind our backs. The baby was in Aunt Shakuntala's room, watched over by the midwife who helped it out of Shanti's womb, but there was no doubt that everyone at the wedding knew that Shanti had already given birth to a bastard. The baby couldn't be hidden forever, but right now, Aunt Shakuntala couldn't bear the thought of people looking at the child and making sly comments.

Nandini walked around with a faint smile and arched eyebrows, frequently whispering to small groups of women. Aunt Shakuntala missed Sanu, who'd wanted to come but had been held back by final exams. Had Sanu been here, she could at least have drawn some comfort from him.

"The groom is a good man," Aunt Shakuntala heard her husband tell some guests. They nodded, their eyes flickering toward Lamfu, who sat on a couch next to Shanti near the buffet table. Shanti's head was lowered, her bright red sari over her forehead so that her face was hidden.

A neighbor woman came up to Aunt Shakuntala and said, "Now you'll have little ones running in this yard. Don't forget to invite us for the bhoj. Such delicious food."

Aunt Shakuntala couldn't tell whether the woman was laughing at her.

After the guests left, Shanti and Lamfu moved into their room, the very room where Aunt Shakuntala had slept only a few months ago. In the hallway, she sat on the floor, exhausted, and complained to Mohandas in a weepy voice that she would not be able to bear seeing them together every day.

Mohandas answered, "The problem is solved. She's your daughter, and that child is your grandson." His eyes softened. "Shakuntala, what is written in fate always happens. Why do you fight it so hard?"

She was silent for a moment. Then she said, slowly, "What did I do to deserve this?" The softness in his eyes vanished. "It's always about you, isn't it?" And he left the house. Her mind, slow and tired, told her that he thought she was a silly old woman.

Lamfu seemed content with his new role. Most of the time he stayed with the baby, carrying him around the house, talking to him in some incomprehensible language probably he himself did not understand. He did all the housework willingly, as if he were a servant. To Aunt Shakuntala's horror, one day she even found him washing her clothes in the yard. She quickly snatched away her underwear, disgusted that he had touched it. He stared at her in confusion.

Whenever he looked at Shanti, he smiled, and his yellow teeth showed. Aunt Shakuntala tried to see, from her daughter's face, how Shanti felt about him. But Shanti seemed to have no opinion of his looks and treated him as she might an old and respectful servant; she watched him when he talked to and comforted the baby, and she maintained her distance.

What she did with Lamfu at night puzzled Aunt Shakuntala. Did she sleep close to him, or did she turn the other way so as not to see his face?

The child was healthy and strong, and he was seemed to grow by the hour. He was already three months old. Sometimes, when Aunt Shakuntala peeked into the other room, she found Shanti looking at him adoringly or telling him a story as if he could understand. Aunt Shakuntala found herself studying his face, how his cheeks dimpled when he smiled. But then she told herself she'd have no part of it. She never offered to hold him or to change his soiled clothes, even though she did, at times, have an urge to touch him, some soft part of him, as if to verify his existence.

Sometimes when Aunt Shakuntala's eyes met Shanti's, she

would try to peer inside her daughter, to learn what she was thinking, to see whether she was suffering. But to her amazement Aunt Shakuntala saw in her daughter's eyes not pain but fortitude and a slowly growing sense of satisfaction.

In Nandini, surprisingly, Aunt Shakuntala finally found some solace. As a woman, she understood Aunt Shakuntala's emotions and the shame brought by her daughter. "I know how you feel, Aunt Shakuntala," Nandini said in the kitchen, where they were sitting. She placed her hand on Aunt Shakuntala's. "You never got what you deserve."

Aunt Shakuntala knew Nandini was referring to Mohandas, and she felt toward her a warmth she'd believed she could feel only for her children. They talked about Sanu, and how tall and handsome he was. Sanu had visited after his final exams and held the baby in his arms. The baby had soiled himself, and Sanu had laughed. He had even joked with Lamfu. Aunt Shakuntala had been irritated by the comfortable manner in which Sanu interacted with the couple, but she didn't say anything.

After Nandini left, Aunt Shakuntala prayed for a long time in the puja room, asking Lord Krishna that her son become a great man. She also wanted to say something to Krishna about Shanti and her baby, but the proper words did not come. As she was leaving the puja room, she bumped into Shanti, whose cheeks were rosy with rouge and whose lips were covered with lipstick. Aunt Shakuntala was startled; Shanti looked like a grown woman.

"What are you doing?" Aunt Shakuntala asked harshly.

"Asking for God's blessing," Shanti said, and shoved past her mother.

All through the evening, Aunt Shakuntala was troubled, unable to understand her daughter's appearance. When Mohandas came home, she suggested they build a small hut behind the house for Lamfu and Shanti. Her husband, humming his religious tunes, listened to her and, when she finished talking, said, "We'll have to wait. We don't have the money." And he went to sleep.

Aunt Shakuntala woke late that night to the sound of laughter from the other room. First it was Shanti's voice, squealing, followed by a slow *heh, heh, heh* from Lamfu. Then, after a short silence, Aunt Shakuntala heard a shuffling noise. She glanced at the clock beside her bed; it was two o'clock.

"I can't sleep," she said loudly, hoping Mohandas would hear, but he was sound asleep, his face close to her shoulder. She got up, put on her slippers, and quietly shuffled down the hallway. Their door was shut. Aunt Shakuntala stood outside, listening to the squeals and grunts. She softly pushed the door open about two inches. Shanti and Lamfu were intertwined in bed, the outlines of their bodies merging into each other's. Shanti moaned, and Lamfu said something to comfort her.

Aunt Shakuntala returned to her bed, her knees weak. Mohandas was sleeping in the same position. She lay next to him, then moved closer and placed a hand on his shoulder. His nose twitched and, mumbling something, he turned to face the wall. She tugged at his hip, hoping he'd turn back toward her. He didn't move. Aunt Shakuntala took her hand away. Suddenly pressure rose in her throat, and in her attempt to stifle it, she let out a cry.

Mohandas woke. "What's the matter?"

Aunt Shakuntala's eyes welled up with tears.

"Are you not feeling well?" he asked and put his hand on her forehead. Aunt Shakuntala kept looking at him. Then she closed her eyes.

The Man with Long Hair

THE MAN with long hair appeared around the street corner, his self-confidence apparent even from a distance. And that long, jet-black hair—obviously he combed and oiled it every day. It remained unruffled even in the monsoon wind that had started that morning. Everyone on the street—housewives shopping for fresh vegetables, elderly men taking their walk, teenagers with their dogs, street vendors heating the first oil of the day—made way for him almost instinctively. He was tall and slender, somewhat effeminate.

The man passed beneath Aditya's apartment and disappeared at the next corner, toward Kesar Mahal. Aditya knew the man was heading toward the National Dance House for his morning rehearsals—Aditya had seen him in the play *Malati Madan* the week before. Aditya moved from the window to his worn-out sofa, which he had purchased from a relative. It creaked as he sat down.

He knew his wife, Shobha, was watching him. She was sweeping the floor of the kitchen, an extension of the bedroom, but she had been eyeing him when he stood by the window. She pushed aside the old bedsheet that separated the bedroom from the tiny bathroom and swept the dust into a neat little mound and deftly shoveled it onto a sheet of newspaper. After she folded the paper into a small package, she threw it out the kitchen window, where the morning light was seeping in. A week ago, a pedestrian had knocked on their door, a crumpled newspaper in his hand, his right shoulder sprinkled with dust. Aditya had tried to calm the man, but he walked away, warning, "The next time, the police will come." Aditya had scolded Shobha, but she said, "There's no other place to throw. Everyone does it."

Now she came toward him, avoiding his eyes. "Will you drink some tea?" she asked in her soft voice.

She was shy by nature, and although he hadn't minded that when his mother was alive, now her shyness frequently irritated him. "Tea, tea. That's all you can think of," he said. "So many things are happening in this world. Governments falling. People dying of cholera and other diseases. Wild animals roaming the cities. And all you can come up with is tea." He knew his diatribe was unreasonable, but he didn't like the way she had watched him when he stood by the window.

She twisted a corner of her dhoti in her fingers. The pockmarks on her face became more noticeable as she blushed.

He felt sorry, and motioned with his hand for her to bring the tea.

Aditya had been thinking about the man with long hair ever since seeing him in *Malati Madan*. The man lived in a guest house, along with the rest of the cast members, on the adjacent street. Aditya knew this because he saw the man every morning, at seven, walking alone to the theater for rehearsals and returning to the guest house at noon. The other actors walked as a group, talking and laughing. It appeared that the man wanted nothing to do with them.

After bringing his tea, Shobha went into the bathroom with a pile of dirty clothes in her arms. Aditya sat on the bed and sipped, trying to understand why his mind was dwelling on the man with long hair. It was not a sexual feeling; he knew that. It was more like an obsession, a gnawing obsession. It seemed as if he'd known the man somewhere, but he couldn't tell where. Had the man featured in Aditya's past life? Aditya didn't believe in such nonsense, so he dismissed the thought.

He had been shaving in the bathroom that Saturday morning last week when his wife said, "Did you hear?" Her voice, as always, was barely audible. He pretended not to hear. She spoke again, a bit louder. "There's a new theater group in town. They're playing *Malati Madan* at the National Dance House this month. I was thinking, if you . . ."

He glanced at her reflection in the portable mirror on the glass counter above the sink, but all he could see was her forehead and her left eye. She had just come back from Pashupatinath Temple, and a large tika was etched on her forehead. Only two weeks ago, she had asked him for two rupees to go see the film *Taangewali*, which starred her favorite actor, Jitendra. She knew it was a lot; he made little money as a teacher at the local school, which had shut down for summer holidays.

He was about to say no when he nicked himself. Cursing, he shoved his hand into his trouser pocket and tossed a fifty-rupee note at her. She knelt and picked up the money, looking with concern at the trickle of blood running down his neck. Then, before he could stop himself, he said, "I'll go with you." His reflection in the mirror registered surprise. He didn't like theater, nor did he like films. He never understood how people could sit through three hours of nonsense, wasting their time and money.

Later, he realized he may have felt sorry for her, having to go to those silly films by herself. Occasionally, he did feel guilty about neglecting his wife; even the old woman in the apartment downstairs had pointed this out to him. "Ever since your mother died," the old woman said, one hand on her hip while they stood on the landing, "you have been treating her as if she doesn't exist. Aditya, I'm telling you, your mother is very unhappy up there." She pointed toward the heavens. Soon after Aditya and Shobha's wedding, Aditya's mother had passed away, after which Aditya started losing interest in Shobha. He reasoned to himself that it wasn't his fault. He had married only because his mother had forced him to. He had kept putting off marriage until his mother, in protest, refused to get up from her bed. Raising her sad eyes to the ceiling, as if she were carrying on a private conversation with God, she declared, "I will die without the pleasure of a daughter-in-law."

He finally relented, and after Shobha came into the house, he found that, despite himself, he liked her soft voice and the way her hair smelled like a garden after rain. But something held him back. He made love to her only occasionally, and then out of a sense of duty. He kept his conversations with her to a minimum. This was easy when his mother was alive, because his mother kept Shobha busy with household chores. At night in bed she had an expectant look on her face, as if she wished he'd talk to her, recount the day's events, complain about someone. Even when they made love, all he did was grunt and groan.

After his mother died, Aditya found that he did not even want to look at Shobha's face when he got up in the morning, and he hated being seen with her in public. Whenever they did go out, she piled on too much makeup and stayed close to him, her sticky hand grasping his. He talked to her only when crossing streets ("Watch out for that car") or when deciding whether to eat potato patties or water crunches from street stalls. If he tried to talk to her, the conversation was inevitably superficial — some comment about politics (gleaned through his assiduous reading of the daily newspaper) or about something in which she was not interested—and he would grow even more irritated. Once in a while, she would look longingly at a child playing on the streets and back at him. He'd stopped making love to her because he couldn't arouse himself. At times she tried to stimulate him with her hand, but the more she tried, the more the whole thing disgusted him, and he pushed her away. She'd turn the other way and sigh heavily before falling asleep.

"Two years already, Aditya, and no child," the old woman downstairs had said. "Is something wrong? With you? With her?"

That Saturday evening, after the lights dimmed in the theater and the curtains opened, Aditya regretted having come. Every seat in the theater was filled, and body odor hovered in the air. A child in the row behind kicked Aditya's seat, and a woman close by talked in a whiny voice to her husband. Aditya's back became stiff.

Malati Madan was one of the oldest and the most popular Nepali musicals; it was performed in the local theaters at least four or five times a year, and he could not remember how many times his mother had taken him to see it. His wife had probably seen it even more often, but the way her gleaming eyes were fixed on the stage, one would think this was the first time she had been to theater. Even as the play opened, Aditya contemplated making some excuse and going outside for a smoke, but then he saw the man who was playing the part of Madan. He lay prostrate on the stage floor, mourning the loss of his dead Malati. A solitary, dim light barely illuminated his body. Aditya, to his surprise, was moved.

The music started, and the actor stood, gradually turning his face toward the audience as the spotlight brightened and the harmonium grew louder. Finally, the music reached a crescendo, filling the large auditorium with the plaintive wail of the harmonium and sitar. He sang:

> Alas, my beloved Malati,
> Alas, my missing heart.
> What have you done to me?
> You were the soul of my past season.
> This season my soul is lost among the trees.

But it was not his singing that made Aditya breathless. It was the man's presence: his mournful eyes, aristocratic nose, slender hands gesticulating in sadness. It was his broad royal forehead, his long shining hair, which fell down his back. Aditya had an almost uncontrollable desire to rush up to the stage and touch the man, say something to him—he didn't know what. He clutched the armrest. Intent on watching the stage, Shobha didn't notice his tension.

For the rest of the play, it was as if the actor were speaking directly to him, as if Aditya were the lost beloved Malati, abandoned in a world devoid of color and charm.

The play ended with Madan drinking poison, singing to Malati until his tongue could no longer move:

> Alas, my beloved,
> Alas, my missing heart.
> Why did you even think I could
> live without you?
> Could a flower survive without
> its lover bee?
> Would a moth want to live
> without its killer light?
> So I am coming to you, beloved Malati.
> Wait, I am coming to reclaim my soul.

Aditya's wife was quietly sniffling when the curtains closed. For a moment, Aditya sat there, wanting to laugh at himself.

But before he had a chance to think too much, he said, "Let's go." He took Shobha's hand and rushed her out of the auditorium, bumping and shoving people in his way. "Idiot," shouted an old man with a cane. "Such a beautiful play, and he can't wait to leave."

Once they reached the apartment, Aditya asked his wife to make herself dinner and to leave him alone.

She looked at him searchingly. "You didn't like the play?"

He made a vague gesture and reached in his pocket for a cigarette.

Around ten o'clock, Shobha finished the dishes and came to bed. She had a wounded expression and wouldn't look at him as she slid under the blanket.

As she began softly snoring in her sleep, Aditya noticed beads of perspiration on her upper lip. The pockmarks were obscured by the dim lamp, and her hair was strewn on the pillow and on her breasts, moving up and down as she breathed.

His hand hovered over her. He had an urge to touch her, but he didn't want to wake her, lest she think he was initiating something and expect more. Suddenly the room felt hot, and he reached for the fan. As the cool air brushed his face, he looked at her again. A strand of hair rustled on her forehead. He leaned over, planning to kiss her so lightly that she wouldn't know, but she abruptly opened her eyes. His heart pounding, he brushed something imaginary from her cheeks. "A fly," he said.

She reached for her face, momentarily alarmed; then she smiled. "I was dreaming about the play," she whispered. "You were Madan, and I was Malati, and you sang to me."

"It's just a play," he said, but he couldn't help smiling.

They made love, a surprise to both of them. It had been so long that Aditya felt like a novice. As he clumsily entered her, grunting, she made sounds like a cat in distress. He clutched her hair, sometimes tugging at it so hard that she cried out in pain.

Later, after she had fallen asleep, he went to the window and watched the rain storming down in a torrent. A street light flickered, illuminating the pavement briefly. A drunk crossed the street, the light charting his path in such a zigzag way that he appeared to move in jerks. A young woman in a bright red sari and heavy makeup briefly glanced at Aditya and smiled before turning the corner.

That was a week ago, and since then he had been following the movements of the actor from his window.

He finished his tea and stretched. It was ten o'clock, and the sun was shining directly through the window. Shobha was beating clothes against the bathroom floor, the heavy *thump, thump* ringing throughout the building.

When his mother had first brought up the idea of marriage, Aditya said no, he'd never marry. She had ruffled his hair and laughed. Her dear Adi shouldn't talk such nonsense. He had the responsibility of carrying on the name of his father, who had died when Aditya was only eight. And on top of that, she did not know when Lord Shiva was going to call on her to leave this world, and she wanted to see her son with a wife and children before she left. Aditya had few memories of his father: the protective feel of his big palm as they held hands on the street, his whistling every morning while he tied his shoelaces, the strands of black hair sticking out of his nose. As a child, when Aditya saw his friends with their fathers, he felt as if he'd been deprived, and later, when his mother reminded him of his responsibility to the family name, a part of him thought, I hardly knew the man.

Each time his mother showed him photographs of a prospective bride, he feigned interest for her sake. Some of the women were indeed beautiful and came from respectable families; some even came from quite well-to-do families. But none intrigued him. Finally, he said yes to the photograph of Shobha, despite the pockmarks on her face. The only reason he had picked her, he later understood, was the sight of her shy, timid eyes and soft chin; she didn't appear the type to ask too much of anyone.

He often wondered why she had agreed to the marriage. Aditya himself was not an attractive man. He was short and thin, almost emaciated. He had a crooked nose—for which he had been taunted as a child—set off with thick eyebrows and cloudy eyes. He had always been conscious of being unattractive, and now he wondered whether this was the reason he found himself obsessed by, even envious of, the beautiful man with the long hair. But it was more than envy, Aditya knew. The man had surfaced because he had something to pass on to Aditya, something that had to do with how Aditya was living his life.

Aditya went to the National Dance House early the next morning to buy a ticket for another show, this time just for himself. The woman behind the counter was reading a cheap Hindi novel, and he had to tap twice on the counter to get her attention. She slowly removed her eyes from the book and looked at him.

"One for tonight," he said, pushing twenty rupees across the counter.

"It's twenty-five," she said. "The price went up."

He gave her the money and pocketed the ticket, but hesitated for a moment.

"What now?"

"What's his name?" he blurted. "The one with the long hair?"

"All actors have long hair these days," she said. "Which one?"

"Madan," Aditya said, looking around to make sure no one heard him. A couple had entered the lobby.

"Oh, that one," she said with a smile. "Can't you read? Right there." She pointed to a handwritten poster behind his back.

Nirmal Kumar. Aditya read the name slowly.

Just then some men came into the lobby through a side door marked NO ENTRY, arguing about some lighting problem during last night's show. They threw him a glance and resumed their discussion. One of them lit a cigarette and went to talk with the woman behind the counter.

Making sure no one was watching him, Aditya opened the side door and found himself in a narrow, dimly lit corridor. He walked through and ended up backstage, facing a couple of doors. Makeup rooms, he imagined. At first he considered turning back, but when he saw no one in the area, he became curious. To his right was the stage, lit by a bright spotlight on the ceiling. As he went through a small side opening, the spotlight threw the shadow of the seats across the side walls, making them look like tall people appraising him, with his arms dangling awkwardly by his sides.

He paced the stage for a few moments. Then he lay down on the floor, propped up on one elbow, and gesturing with his hand. He whispered, trying not to laugh:

> Could a flower survive without
> its lover bee?
> Would a moth want to live
> without its killer light?

He stood up just as the door from the lobby opened, bringing in a shaft of light and a human figure. Aditya wanted to run and hide backstage, but that might have given the impression that he was stealing something. So he stayed where he was, in the middle of the stage, his hands in his pockets, and watched the figure approach.

It was the man with long hair. Today, his hair was untied and waved slightly as he walked. He came to a stop in front of the stage and looked at Aditya. "You're the new actor? Where's your script?" His voice was high and feminine.

"Script?" Aditya said.

The man stroked his nose and said, "They didn't give you a script yet? Maybe that moron took it with him. Imagine, quitting right in the middle of our tour. And he wasn't that good either. Where did they find you?"

Aditya jumped off the stage and stood in front of him. "I'm sorry," he said.

"What are you sorry for?" Nirmal said. He leaned against the stage and lit a cigarette. "It's not your fault they dragged you into this." He sighed and looked up at the ceiling, then back at Aditya. "Go get a script from the so-called director," Nirmal said. "He's probably boozing it up in that bar across the street. I'll show you what needs to be done."

"I have to leave," Aditya said, and quickly made his way up the aisle.

"Don't worry," the long-haired man shouted. "It's an easy part."

Aditya stood outside the theater, his heart pounding. For a moment, the sights and sounds around him became strangely lucid: the blaring horns, cries of vendors, pestering beggars, the unruly children and their concerned mothers, the movement of the cars, the sunlight flickering on Queen's Pond a hundred yards away.

He walked home, unable to understand what was happening. Now he seriously considered what had occurred to him before: that he may have had some connection with the actor in a past life. Nothing else could explain his obsession, the incredible energy he felt in his body at this moment.

At home, he found his photo album and looked at the pictures of his childhood. Aditya was a timid-looking child, always holding the hand of either his father or his mother. His mother was a chubby, matronly woman. His father was tall and thin, with a heavy mustache and laughing eyes. Aditya scrutinized his father's face, noting that he himself didn't have his father's strong chin and laughing manner.

Before the performance that evening, Aditya set out his best trousers and shirt.

"Where are you going?" Shobha asked.

"To visit some friends," he said, ignoring her quizzical look.

He ironed the shirt and trousers while she watched him from the kitchen. Once dressed, he combed his hair in front of the bathroom mirror. Her face appeared behind him in the mirror. "Dinner?" she said. "Will you eat?"

"I'm not hungry right now," he said. "You can go ahead and eat."

On the landing downstairs he saw the old lady, who immediately blocked his way and said, "Where to?"

"A friend's house," he said.

"Hmmmm," she said but didn't step aside. "When does your school start?"

"In about two weeks."

He tried to move past her, but she wouldn't budge. "You have too much free time on your hands," she said.

Aditya glanced at his watch. The show was to start in ten minutes. "Old witch," he muttered under his breath.

"What was that?" She looked him up and down. "Aditya, I'm

telling you. Take that wife of yours out with you. Otherwise
one day she'll go crazy."

"Get out of my way, Sharda-Ma."

"You should be having a child, but here you are, gallivanting
around town by yourself—"

"Old woman, will you get out of my way?"

Because he was late, he had to sit at the back of the theater.
Right in front of him sat a man with a neck as thick as a bull's.
As the light dimmed, Aditya tilted his head to the side and heard
a woman behind him mutter, "What is he? A camel?" When
Nirmal came onstage, Aditya held his breath. Nirmal was beau-
tiful, his eyes outlined in kohl, his lips reddened with lipstick.

As he started to sing, someone in the audience shouted,
"Madan is a faggot," eliciting both laughter and demands for
quiet. Nirmal glanced in the direction of the voice and continued his song. The brief distraction didn't affect the beauty of his
singing, and, again, Aditya felt a stirring within him.

"Madan likes men," the same voice rang out, this time
louder, more menacing.

"Be quiet," a woman shouted.

"Madan is a faggot." This time there were two, three voices.
The singing began to falter. "Madan is a faggot."

The activities on the stage stopped. Nirmal glared in the
direction of the noise.

Aditya stood up and, bumping past other people's knees,
made his way toward the voices, a slow anger filling him. The
lights came on, and there was a collective groan from the audience. A couple of elderly men argued with the young men, who
were now seated but laughing.

"What kind of behavior is this?" one of the old men said.
Aditya recognized him as the man with the cane who had

shouted at him when he'd rushed out of the theater with his wife.

"What's the problem?" Aditya said, his heart pounding.

Sensing trouble, some people had started to leave.

"There's no problem," replied one of the young men, a tall lanky fellow with a hooked nose. "Who said there's a problem?"

"What is the problem?" A rotund man wearing a tie approached.

"Who are you?" the young man asked.

"The manager," the man said. More people hovered around the scene while many stood near the exit, watching. The harmonium player must have accidentally touched the keys; there was, for one brief moment, a soft wail.

The young men looked at each other in mock surprise. "What happened? Is there a problem? What's the problem?"

"Please," the manager said. "Let the show continue. If you don't like the show, please leave."

"Madan is a faggot!" one of the young men shouted.

Aditya looked at the stage, where Nirmal was whispering to another actor. Some people in the audience laughed.

"You," Aditya said loudly to the young man, his voice shaking. "Come outside and settle this with me. You want to insult a great actor?" He had no idea where his bravery had come from. He had never in his life initiated a fight.

The three young men jumped up. "Why outside?" one said. "We'll settle you right here." He landed a solid blow on the side of Aditya's neck, making him reel and fall on the lap of a woman who screamed and pushed him away. He landed on the floor, twisting his right knee, and was pummeled by blows and kicks. First, he felt sharp, suffocating pain in his abdomen, then an excruciating seizure in his throat, as if someone were ripping it open. "Motherfucker," "pig," "ass." Words floated around him, disembodied voices that came from near and far at once. He could tell that some people were coming to his rescue, and the manager's voice rang out, "These hoodlums!" For an instant his head cleared, and he saw pandemonium in the hall: people pushing and shoving one another to get out. One of the young men, his shirttail hanging out, was tussling with the manager. Someone aimed another kick at Aditya's head, but this time he blocked it with his hands. His face was wet, but when he touched his lips and his nose, he couldn't feel them. A black boot loomed above his face, and a stark, white light flashed in front of him. His nose bubbled.

When he came to, Nirmal was holding him. "It's okay; don't worry," Nirmal said. A white object like a butterfly floated before Aditya's face, and he realized that Nirmal was offering him a handkerchief. Clutching it, Aditya struggled to his feet. "Where are they?" he asked, the words coming out of him in a gurgle.

"They ran away."

"We'd better take him to the hospital," the manager said.

Aditya shook his head. His knee hurt, and his face felt as if it were being pressed by a bulldozer. He dabbed his nose with the handkerchief and said, "No need for the hospital. I'll just go home."

"In this state?" Nirmal said. "Why did you do that? You're obviously not made for fights."

Aditya laughed. "And you are?"

"I know karate," Nirmal said.

Most of the audience had already left, but some people still milled around, talking in excited voices, analyzing the incident.

"What happened to the show?" Aditya said.

"It's over," Nirmal said. "Where do you live?"

"Paknajol."

"I live in Samakhusi. Come, I'll walk you home." He paused. "In case those men are waiting for you outside."

Nirmal arranged Aditya's arm over his shoulders and led him out. He asked Aditya again whether he wanted to go to the hospital, and Aditya said no. "You are stubborn," Nirmal said. They started toward Paknajol, Aditya limping and leaning on Nirmal. When they passed under a streetlight, Aditya noticed that Nirmal still wore his makeup. His hair was tied behind with a rubber band. "You're a good actor," Aditya told him.

Nirmal shrugged.

For a moment, Aditya couldn't believe he was walking home with this man. Although his body hurt, he felt pleasure and relief.

As they neared his apartment, Aditya said, "I need a drink."

"I don't drink."

"Then keep me company."

Nirmal hesitated, then said, laughing, "Okay, but don't get drunk in this state."

They entered a small bar in Thamel. When the waiter brought Aditya a glass of the local whiskey, Aditya told Nirmal, "I feel as if I know you from somewhere else."

"You saw me this morning," Nirmal said with a wry smile. "I thought you were the substitute. And you didn't correct me."

"No, no," Aditya said. "That's not what I meant." But he couldn't explain it. What could he say? That he knew Nirmal from their past lives?

The whiskey made his cheeks warm, and he wanted to order another, but Nirmal said, with some authority, "Enough. You need rest."

When they stepped outside, the sky grumbled and roared. Large drops of rain fell on their heads and clattered on the surrounding roofs. They ran, Aditya limping and holding on to

Nirmal's arm. The apartment was only two blocks away, so they stayed under the awnings of the shops, dashing in and out of the rain.

By the time they reached the apartment, both were soaked and laughing. Aditya asked Nirmal to come inside until the rain calmed down. "I'm already wet," Nirmal said, but he followed Aditya upstairs.

When Shobha opened the door and saw Aditya's condition, she gasped. "What happened? Who did this to you?"

Aditya placed his hand on her shoulder and said, "It's no big deal. Look who's come for a visit." But Shobha ran to the bathroom, paying no attention to the actor. Aditya looked at Nirmal sheepishly. Shobha came back with a towel and a bottle of iodine, and forced Aditya to sit on the sofa. She dabbed the iodine on his face, making him wince. "You've been drinking," she said.

"Not much," Nirmal said. "Just a glass."

She went to the bathroom and brought back another towel for Nirmal. Now she looked at him more closely. "Oh, it's you," she said, finally recognizing him. She glanced at Aditya with some irritation, then asked Nirmal where he had found her husband. When Nirmal explained what had happened, she scolded Aditya. "Who asked you to be the hero? And why did you go to see the play again?"

Aditya was surprised by her tone of authority. "We have such a great actor in our house," Aditya said with a laugh, "and all you can do is harass me."

"I don't care." She turned to Nirmal. "I guess I should thank you. Do you want tea?"

Nirmal said that he ought to get going and pack for the next day, as the theater company was moving to a different town. Aditya placed his hand on the actor's and said, "Please, just one cup. There's time."

When his wife went to the kitchen, Nirmal whispered, "You've got a nice wife."

Aditya smiled. "Usually she's very shy."

"You never can tell with women," Nirmal said.

"Are you married?"

"No," Nirmal said with a mischievous smile. "I can't stay with one woman. I tend to like all of them."

"Why can't you stay with one?"

"Who knows? Maybe it's just my nature." He loosened his hair from the rubber band, deftly combed it with his long slim fingers, then tied it back again.

Aditya wanted to talk to Nirmal about his own self-consciousness, but didn't know how to broach the topic. Instead, he went to the cupboard and took out the family album. He sat down and flipped through the pages. The pain in his knee and face began to fade. "See," he said, pointing to a family picture that showed him in the city park, holding his parents' hands.

"Is that you?" Nirmal said, laughing.

"Who else?" Aditya said.

Shobha came back with tea and said, "What's this? Looking at pictures at this hour?"

Nirmal said to her, "Tell me something. Would you have married him had you seen these pictures before your wedding?"

For a moment she blushed, but when she spoke, her voice was firm. "What kind of a question is that? Of course I would have married him. It was written in our fate."

Aditya was surprised at Shobha's confidence in front of a stranger.

The rain was letting up, and they could hear conversations on the street.

Nirmal drank his tea in quick gulps and got up. "Well, you should still have a doctor check you out in the morning."

"Are you coming back to the city again?" Aditya asked.

"Not for a while," Nirmal said and, bidding them good night, left.

The next morning Aditya sat by the window. The cast and the crew of the play appeared on the street corner, laughing and joking. Nirmal was last, walking alone, carrying a suitcase. When he passed Aditya's apartment building, he glanced up at the window. Aditya waved at him, then shouted, "The next time you're here, come for tea in my house."

Nirmal nodded and moved on.

Aditya's wife came and stood next to him. "Who is it?" she asked. When she saw Nirmal walking away, she said, "Good riddance." She had just come out of the bath, and he could smell mustard oil in her hair. He moved closer and breathed her in. Then he licked her ear, and she jerked away from the window with a giggle. She blushed. "People will see. What has come over you this early in the morning?"

This World

THEY MET in New Jersey at a wedding party. Jaya knew the bride, a young Brahmin woman of twenty-four from Kathmandu, and Kanti was taking a course in economics at New York University with the bridegroom, a Nepali professor twenty years older than the bride. It was an arranged marriage, and Kanti had heard that the bride's parents had given away their daughter to the older professor in order to get their green cards.

On the professor's lawn, Kanti was in line at the buffet table, wondering whether she could slip away soon after eating, when she noticed the man in front of her. He was tall, with an appealing face, and he was fair, so fair that she thought he was European. He had bushy eyebrows, with two strands of white hair growing out of each in perfect symmetry. He saw her looking at him and said, in Nepali, "Yes, yes, I am a Nepali." The words tumbled out thickly, as if he didn't speak the language often. "Did you come here with someone?" he asked, with a familiarity that made it seem he already knew her. When she answered, "By myself," he said, "Then we should eat together. Over there." He pointed to a secluded corner. Their bodies touched as they scooped up the food.

She joined him in the corner, and they ate, standing. After some silence, he said, again in English, "Well, aren't you going to tell me about yourself? I thought that's what this is all about."

"This?" she asked.

"Yes, you and I are going to be lovers."

She laughed. "You are very arrogant."

"You'll come to like that about me."

She realized that they were conversing entirely in English, but it didn't seem odd, as it often did when she talked in English with other Nepalis in America. It was as if he thought in English.

He brought her a glass of wine, then another, then another. Each time, she told herself this was the last one, that she'd leave his company and go talk to someone else, or leave the party, as she'd originally planned. But as the evening progressed his face became even more arresting, and the conversation unlike conversations she had at Nepali gatherings, which she dreaded attending because they were laden with nostalgia, incessant political chatter, and one-upmanship, with people vying to talk about how much land they owned back home. Talking with Jaya, Kanti could laugh and not worry about how loud it sounded, or whether some senior Nepali gentleman, a professor at a university or a consultant at a firm, would frown at her, or whether the women, with their dark, critical eyes, would talk about how she acted like a loose woman. She couldn't remember how many glasses of wine she'd had, but it didn't matter. She told him how alienated she felt in Kathmandu; how, when she went there two years before, she was like a stranger. She liked the sound of the words and repeated them: "I was a restless ghost in my own country." He put his arm around her and said, "Poor baby," and she thought—her mind floating with wine—He is like me.

She saw him several times that evening in different groups, his long arm visible in the brightness of the fluorescent lamps placed strategically throughout the lawn, his white shirt shining. Once, he winked at her and rolled his eyes at the Nepalis around him, as if in exasperation. She kept wishing he'd come back, talk to her more, but he was laughing with some people he obviously knew. She went to the bride and groom, seated on a couch inside the house, and said goodbye.

A few yards from the house he called her. "I thought we were lovers."

"But you abandoned me," she said.

He came closer. "Never again," he said, then brought his mouth so close to hers that she thought he was about to kiss her. If he had, she didn't know what she'd have done.

He gave her a ride to her apartment in his Volkswagen, his arm waving near her cheeks as he talked. He was born in Nepal, he said, but grew up in Boston, then moved to New York when his parents returned to Kathmandu a few years ago. "But tell me," he asked her, "what's so great about Nepal except for the fact that it's our home country?" He visited Kathmandu every year, hung out with his cousins and friends. "I don't even like the place that much." He smiled at her. "But I love to party there." The word "party" came out of his mouth like a celebration itself. She told him that she was going to Kathmandu that coming summer because her mother was insisting. Occasionally the car drifted to the side of the highway, and in the Lincoln Tunnel he nearly rammed into a truck coming down the other side.

Outside her apartment he took her hand, and her heart thumped. She thought he was going to make a move, but she didn't want to sleep with him, not yet. She found the American sexual mores a bit intimidating. She'd had only two boyfriends during her years here, a German guy she liked but who soon lost interest in her, and a Midwesterner from Ohio, who said he loved her "exotic" eyes. She had had sex with both of them, but not with sufficient passion. In fact, she had a feeling her German boyfriend got bored because she didn't show enough excitement while making love.

But Jaya merely said, "Call me when you reach Kathmandu —I am also going there in May. We'll party together. My father is Somnath Rana." She recognized the name, as he'd meant her to: a minister who'd been involved in a bribery scandal during the Panchayat era, had absconded to the United States, and was now back in Nepal, working for a human rights group. He wrote down his New York phone number. "For rainy days."

The next morning she couldn't find the slip of paper. She looked for his name in the phonebook, but it wasn't listed. She got in touch with a few acquaintances from the party, but none knew him, and the bride and groom were already honeymooning in Hawaii. Gradually, she began to see his face in the subway in the faces of other young men who were also fair and lanky—and arrogant. Once a young Italian, who saw her staring at him, swaggered up to her and said, "Hey, you're cute. You Indian?"

In May she got her master's degree in economics and made preparations to go to Nepal. She left most of her belongings in the apartment with her roommate. "I don't think I can stay there too long," Kanti said. When her roommate asked how she was going to get a new visa, she said, "I'm applying to Duke. Let's see what happens."

When her feet touched the tarmac of Tribhuvan International Airport, in Kathmandu, the wind, coupled with the sight of her mother waving frantically from the terminal, brought back memories of how lonely she'd been the last time she was here, two years earlier. As soon as she and her mother reached the house in Paknajol, she looked up Jaya's father's name in the directory. There it was: Somnath Rana, Jawalakhel. Her finger lingered on the name. Her mother, who had set something to cook in the kitchen and come back, asked whom she was looking for.

"Just a friend," Kanti answered.

Her mother talked incessantly, as if she had been holding her breath until her daughter came home. Kanti noticed new lines in her face and the way her eyes seemed smaller.

They agreed to meet at a bar in a hotel.

She found him at a table, drinking Jack Daniel's. "I hate this country," he said. "I don't know why I came." Because he laughed as he said this, she heard no bitterness in the comment. "Look at them; just look at them. Pathetic." He shook his head as he surveyed the bar, full of Nepali men in business suits and young men and women in jeans. Later, on the dance floor, he kissed her impulsively, his wet lips nearly suffocating her, and she wondered whether she should have come to the bar to meet him. But he danced wildly, and soon she found herself matching his movements, laughing, enjoying the way the colorful revolving lights cast patterns on his face.

He didn't drink anymore that evening, and they left the hotel in his Suzuki to roam the city. They drove toward Ring Road, and he parked the jeep in a secluded spot. "I knew you would call me," he said. When she asked how he knew, he replied, "You're a lonely soul." And when he embraced her and kissed her again, she didn't resist; when he started caressing her breasts, she let him. They made love in the back seat, giggling when the headlight of an occasional car shone on them.

★

They spent long afternoons in expensive hotel rooms in the city. He had money—his father owned land all over the country— so she didn't worry about how often he opened his wallet.

In a hotel one drowsy afternoon, lying next to Jaya, Kanti played with a long gray strand of hair among the thicket on his chest. She twisted it, tugged at it, resisting the temptation to break it off. "Ouch!" he said, and it struck her that he didn't say "Aiya," as a Nepali would. "You want to bring me bad luck, Kanti?" he said, laughing. "Who knows what could happen in this godforsaken country." He climbed on top of her and un-abashedly told her about his fantasies: standing by the door, watching her make love to another man; coming home to find her seducing another woman. She did not find these fantasies particularly exciting, but she willingly responded when she felt him inside her.

Often, he fell asleep soon after they made love. She would stand by the window, figuring it must be cold outside, because the beggars were bundled up on the pavement. She could imagine the city of Kathmandu like New York, covered with snow, cars coming to a standstill, the Queen Pond frozen, the ice on top reflecting the light that burned at its periphery all night.

Her mother appeared perplexed. She'd heard rumors, Kanti was sure, that her daughter had had relationships with boys in America. But perhaps she didn't think that she'd see someone so openly here. "What has happened to you?" she asked Kanti one afternoon, her eyes filled with resentment. "You were not like this before. Mrs. Sharma from the neighborhood was asking me if having a boyfriend was all you learned in America."

"Jaya is different," Kanti said.

"He is too much like those Americans."

Kanti smiled. Mother's knowledge of Americans was limited to the tourists she saw on the streets of the city.

The neighbors and relatives stared at Jaya when they saw him and Kanti together, as if he were indeed a kuirey, an American. Kanti assumed that was because he walked with a swagger, his chest challenging the world. And he went for days without shaving. Sometimes his jeans looked as if they had not been washed in weeks.

Jaya's friends in the city were richer than Kanti's friends. His cousins and best friends, Sunil and Vikas, copied Jaya's nonchalance, his accent, and the dreamy way he talked about himself and America. Unlike his cousins, his other friends were not from the fallen Rana aristocracy. One was the son of the owner of a big hotel; another, the son of a man who owned major sugar factories and a Honda dealership. Often, when sitting in an expensive restaurant in the Soaltee Hotel or Yak & Yeti Hotel, or when watching Jaya and his friends play cricket in the enormous compound of Jaya's house, Kanti could scarcely believe the world into which she'd stumbled—the world of upper-class Nepalis. She liked the ease with which they moved in their surroundings, with which they traveled back and forth between America and Nepal, between Europe and Nepal. At parties in Jaya's house, she heard them talk about building new hotels in the city, about the new BMWs they'd bought, or how they'd just come back from a shopping spree in London.

Jaya's parents barely spoke to her, not because they disliked her but because they seemed unaware of her presence. Sometimes Kanti felt inadequate, as if she were a poor cousin, and she clung to Jaya.

At a party one evening, while the monsoon rain sounded like a riot outside, she was standing alone in a corner, watching Jaya talk to his friends across the room, when a middle-aged woman she recognized as Jaya's cousin came over and spoke to her. "You take him seriously, don't you?" the woman asked, and before Kanti could respond, she warned, "Be careful, Kanti. You don't know these people. Don't get attached to Jaya."

Kanti wanted her to say more, but the woman gave her a knowing look and moved away.

Kanti thought of her early years in America, how, away from the scrutinizing eyes of her mother and her relatives, she'd initially felt she'd broken free. She went to parties all the time, even smoked pot. She told her American friends how, when she was seventeen, her uncle had seen her walking the streets of Kathmandu holding a boy's hand. Her friends laughed as she mimicked the way he looked her up and down, then did the same to the poor boy. And when she added that her mother hadn't spoken to her for three days, they said, "You're kidding!"

By her fourth year in college, though, she began to pine for home, for the smell of garlic on her mother, the gossip with childhood friends with whom she'd already lost touch, the taste of hot-hot momos, spicy Nepali dumplings. Her American friends didn't understand why she stopped trudging across the campus to go to classes, why she stayed in her room all day with the curtains drawn, why she stopped answering the phone unless the call was from her mother. On the day a friend, Susan, brought her a carrot cake, Kanti said, "I don't feel like eating."

"What's happened to you?"

Kanti couldn't tell her that she hated this country—the way people smiled too much, how everything was always "wonderful," how she didn't feel close to anyone. All she said was that she had a mild bout of homesickness.

"But you've been like this for months now."

Kanti took a small piece of the cake and told Susan she had a headache and needed to sleep.

The day she finished her last exam, she flew back to Nepal not even waiting to get her diploma. But two weeks after she arrived, she wished she were back in America. She couldn't understand why everything in Kathmandu had changed. So much dust, so many houses with their ugly television antennas shooting into the sky, the way people spat on the streets, phlegm shooting out of their mouths, the way they bragged about how much money they had, the way her relatives constantly asked when she was getting married, the way her mother arranged for her to be "viewed" by dull-looking men, the way old men and women stared at her when she walked down the street wearing pants, the way her married friends carried babies in their arms, the way their husbands wore expensive but ill-fitting suits and ordered their wives about in sweet voices. She felt eyes following her everywhere, watching her every move, ready to pounce if she made a false step, didn't speak properly, or addressed someone the wrong way. She became convinced that she couldn't live here, and she despised herself for this, for her consistently critical attitude toward her own people. I live in two worlds, she thought, perched halfway between them. In her restlessness she applied for the master's program at New York University and was accepted.

And now Jaya. He and his friends were playing cricket, and he was giving instructions to one of them who was ready to bat. She caught his eye, and he winked at her, just as he had in New York. She imagined them touring around Europe, or going back to New York to visit old friends, and then, later, back in Nepal with a couple of kids. She wondered where they would live in their old age. In Nepal? It didn't matter. With him, the city had become pleasant. The only thing that worried her was Jaya's drinking. He always had a glass of something in his hand. He was indiscriminate when it came to alcohol: wine, beer, whiskey, rum, even the strong local liquor. Right now he had a glass of gin on the table where she sat.

Jaya and Kanti often went on excursions to the countryside. On his Kawasaki motorbike, he'd come by her house, sometimes deliberately having taken out the muffler so that the noise of the engine shook her quiet neighborhood. As the raucous motorbike stopped outside, Kanti held her breath, a faint throbbing in her throat, and opened the gate. Initially she'd wished Jaya wouldn't do that, but when she saw her neighbors watching from their windows, she gained a sense of satisfaction. Frowning, her mother came to the porch and nodded at Jaya, who gave her an exaggerated greeting, hands held high above his head in namaste. On the next day, her mother would inevitably mutter to her: "These Ranas. The way they flash their money, you'd think they still rule the country. Someone needs to tell them that the Rana rule was over when the people revolted centuries ago."

One afternoon Kanti and Jaya went to Gokarna with a picnic basket. They sat to eat under a large tree. Jaya drank beer and, after two bottles, stroked her face and said, "I haven't felt like this with anyone else."

She called him a liar.

"Seriously," he said.

"So what does it mean?"

He shrugged. "It just means what it means. What are you looking for?"

She shook her head. She already felt too vulnerable.

"I have thought about a life with you," he said.

She waited.

"Don't you have anything to say?" he said.

"It's a serious matter." She swallowed so that her voice wouldn't break.

He reached over and touched her breast.

A voice said, "What is this?" Three men stood a few yards away.

"What do you think this is? Your bedroom?" one of them said.

"What do you want?" Jaya said.

"Who is this?" the man said, pointing to Kanti. "Your sister?" The other two laughed. One of them said, "Sister fucker."

Jaya got up, enraged.

"Jaya, please," Kanti said.

"We like your sister, donkey," another man said. "She's sexy."

Jaya lunged at him. The three men pummeled Jaya, who was trying to protect himself and strike back at the same time. A car appeared in the distance, on the unpaved road that led to the gate. The three men ran off, laughing, shouting, "Your sister is sexy!"

Jaya's mouth was bleeding, and his lower lip and right eye were swollen.

They went to the park's office, where an official took out a first-aid kit and applied iodine to Jaya's wounds. "Those hoodlums," the man said. "Uncontrollable. Two months ago someone was murdered here."

"I remember their faces," Jaya said. "I'll take care of them."

Later, as they walked to the motorcycle, Kanti's heart was still thumping. "We're lucky that car came when it did. Why did you have to fight? And what was that about taking care of them?"

"Hey, I have to protect my sister, don't I?" he said. "My sexy sister."

As summer drew to an end, Jaya brought up the idea of not returning to America for another year or so. He had one more year before completing his graduate degree in business, but, as he said, "I am absolutely in no mood to go back to the books now, Kanti." He wanted to stay in Kathmandu for another three or four months and then maybe go to Europe or even Africa before heading back to the United States. But Kanti had just received word from Duke that she was to be granted an assistantship while working for her Ph.D. in economics. So when Jaya told her he'd decided to stay, Kanti became depressed. She really didn't want to live in Kathmandu any longer. Her mother was becoming more and more critical of her relationship with Jaya. Kanti knew that her mother had in mind another boy, a Brahmin from the city who had just come back from England with a degree in medicine. "You two can get married, then go to America for your Ph.D," her mother said. "Just have one look. You'll like him. I don't know what you see in that hoodlum." The word *hoodlum* touched a nerve in Kanti, and she shouted back at her mother, "He's not a hoodlum. His life is more interesting than yours, you with your 'what will the neighbors say, what will the neighbors think.'" After several minutes of silence, she said, "I want to marry only Jaya, Mother. I won't look at anyone else."

Her mother didn't speak to her for the rest of the day. In the evening, they ate in separate rooms, and Kanti felt a pang of guilt. She had never before shouted at her mother. She went to her mother's room and found her reading the Bhagavad Gita. She gently took the book from her mother's hands and put it aside. "I will see your man," Kanti said, "but you have to give me the option of refusing."

"I know you won't refuse," her mother said. "He's very attractive. Here, let me show you his photograph."

The man had a faint mustache that ran all the way down to his chin. His eyes had a serious quality that she immediately liked, and she had to admit he was not bad looking. "He's okay," she said.

Her mother squeezed her shoulder, saying that she knew her daughter would come around.

"Mother," Kanti warned, "I told you—I might refuse."

"All right, all right," her mother said. "Just a look. After that, it's your decision."

Kanti told her then that she was thinking about taking a year off before starting school again, and staying in Nepal. Her mother said this was a good idea, for she thought that Jaya would be leaving soon to resume his studies. "Once you get married to Prakash—" her mother started, then corrected herself. "If you get married to Prakash, then maybe both of you can go to America."

Kanti walked into a bar in the tourist district of Thamel one afternoon to find Jaya kissing a woman wearing gaudy makeup and a skirt that revealed her thighs. The woman's hand cradled Jaya's neck while Jaya's right hand fondled her breast; their lips were glued together. There was no one else at the bar except the bartender, who was a friend of Jaya's and also knew Kanti. He was polishing a glass, and when he saw Kanti, he froze. Kanti's eyes focused on Jaya's hand, the very hand that she had held, inspected, kissed, and traced with her finger. Dumbfounded, she walked out. She expected to feel angry, but she didn't. She walked the streets of the city for the rest of the afternoon, her body light with shock.

The next day news spread among the people who knew them that Kanti had caught Jaya with another woman. In some versions of the rumor, the woman was a prostitute. Talk of the incident also reached Kanti's mother, who pounded on Kanti's door when she locked herself in her room, "Kanti, open the door. You need to be with someone." Kanti ignored her.

Jaya called later that evening, but she wouldn't speak to him. He came by, this time silently on the motorbike, and her mother shouted at him from the gate. Kanti could see him from the window; his face was grim. What was he thinking? In a short while he left, revving the engine and drowning out her mother's voice.

Kanti avoided everyone for a few days, stayed in her room, listening to music or reading novels she'd already read. She took out her old photo albums and went through the pictures, remembering friends she'd forgotten. One morning, she told her mother that she wanted to go away. Her mother understood. Her daughter needed time, some breathing space, to get over this unspeakable thing, and then she might agree to marry Prakash.

Kanti spent two weeks in India. First, she went to Delhi, visited the Taj Mahal in nearby Agra. She thought of Emperor Shah Jehan, grief-stricken by the death of his beloved queen and wanting to create a grand tomb, which, legend said, engaged the skills of twenty thousand craftsmen for more than twenty years. Kanti sat in the garden by the oblong pool that reflected the tomb. But the dust and the dry, scratchy heat of Agra soon made her want to leave, so she took a train to Bombay. There, she met a high school friend, Sushma, in a girl's hostel near Juhu. Sushma was surprised to see Kanti, especially when she learned that Kanti was traveling by herself. "What? You think you're an American now?" Laughing, Sushma added, "You want to stay in an ashram here? Search for your spiritual self?" The next day, as Kanti was on a train to central Bombay, she saw a couple kissing passionately while the other passengers watched with amusement. A man standing near her prayed, his eyes closed, his chin lifted toward the ceiling. By the time she got off at the bedlam of Victoria Terminus, she was drenched in sweat. She spent the day by the oceanside in Marine Drive, smelling the ocean, and in the evening stopped to observe a street artist draw chalk portraits of gods and goddesses on the sidewalk. Watching the delicate movements of the artist's fingers, the care with which he sharpened the curved trunk of Lord Ganesh, she understood that if she wanted clarity in her life, she'd have to force herself to move beyond Jaya.

Back in Kathmandu, Kanti pushed herself to find a job. Eventually, through an uncle who was with an engineering firm, she found work in a dilapidated office right in the center of the city. The salary was not large, but at least she no longer had to ask her mother for spending money. She started mingling with people again, going to a party in a hotel or attending an afternoon tea on a friend's balcony. Now her mother wanted her to marry as quickly as possible. One night, as Kanti was about to go to bed, her mother told her that Prakash was coming to the house the following week with his two uncles. Kanti didn't protest.

She did sometimes think of Jaya and his self-absorption, his sense of grandeur, and wondered what made him kiss that woman in the bar. How can you be sure, Kanti asked herself, that there isn't something like that in every person, an ugly facet that will at some point reveal itself? How could she be sure, for that matter, that this doctor, this Prakash, did not also have a defect that would surface once they were married?

She did see Jaya twice on social occasions, once at a party in a friend's house, and once in the lobby of the Soaltee Hotel, the very hotel where they'd spent long afternoons. They smiled at each other, self-consciously. Each time it was a different, heavily made-up woman draped around him. Jaya had lost weight, and he looked haggard. She had heard that he was drinking more heavily. At the party, she found him looking at her forlornly from across the room when he probably thought she wouldn't see him.

On the morning Prakash was to arrive, her mother handed her a Banarasi sari she had expressly ordered from India for the occasion. It was beautiful, purple with a red border, embroidered with golden thread.

"Do I really have to wear it?" Kanti said, but before her mother could answer, she got up to try it on, because she hadn't worn a Banarasi in years. The sari suited her, made her face brighter.

"Prakash will be hypnotized," her mother said, her eyes shining.

As the afternoon approached, her mother became nervous and kept scolding the servant for petty mistakes. Kanti was amused, and once she even joked, "Is he coming to see you, Mother?"

Prakash and his two uncles showed up at precisely four o'clock. Both uncles were short, and, on looking closer, Kanti saw that they were twins, although only one had a mustache. Prakash was taller than he had appeared in the picture, with a stoop that made him seem deeply interested in whomever he was talking to. Her mother hurriedly invited them into the drawing room, where a tray of cut apples, bananas, and guavas sat on the table. "Why don't you talk with them, Kanti, while I fetch something from the kitchen," her mother said.

There was silence after her mother left, everyone waiting for someone to initiate a conversation. Kanti knew that the burden was to fall on a man, so she smiled and kept her mouth shut. Finally, the mustached uncle said, "Nice house you have here, Kanti."

Before he could continue, Prakash said, "Is it a master's in economics you have?" His voice was deep and guttural, like that of Amitabh Bacchan, the Hindi movie star.

Kanti nodded.

"Plenty of jobs here with that degree," the mustached uncle said.

They talked about her studies for a while, neither party broaching the crucial question of whether she would indeed go back to America for her Ph.D. if she were to marry Prakash, who had already opened a clinic in the city. Kanti knew that her mother hoped she would forget about the degree once she was married.

Kanti found Prakash easy to talk to. There was a little glimmer in his eyes whenever he said something, as if he, too, found this whole bride-viewing ritual amusing. Soon, the uncles grew quiet and let Prakash and Kanti carry on the conversation. Prakash talked of his experiences in England, the craving for food from home, the loneliness in his dormitory in the evenings, and Kanti felt that he understood what it meant to live in two different worlds.

When her mother brought hot puris and chana-tarkari from the kitchen, the uncles praised her culinary skills. "Our Kanti cooks even better than I do," her mother said, and Kanti looked at her sharply, for she knew how to make only a few dishes, and even then had to ask her mother for help. When Kanti turned, she found Prakash looking at her with a smile to indicate that he could tell what she was thinking.

After they left, her mother praised Prakash so much that Kanti had to tell her to stop. "Well, what did you think?" her mother said. "You liked him, didn't you?"

"He's a nice man," Kanti said. "But I can't make such a momentous decision after just one meeting."

"How many meetings do you need?" Her mother's tone was

somewhat harsh. "This is not America, you know, where you sleep together before marriage."

"That's not what I said. At least a few more meetings, alone, before I can make up my mind."

"You will come across as a very modern girl," her mother said. "They might not like that—the girl saying that she needs to meet the boy more. This doesn't happen here."

"If they don't like it, then maybe I am not right for him."

"Kanti, why are you being so difficult? Here I am, trying and trying, and you never appreciate what I do."

Kanti went to her room, followed by her mother, whose voice had become louder. "You think you can do anything you like, come and go as you please, see as many boys as you want. And now, when such a good man is interested in you—"

"I gave you my decision," Kanti said.

Prakash came to pick her up the next evening in a taxi. She wore a simple salwar-kameez, one of her older ones, from her school days in Nepal.

At the Indian restaurant of the Annapurna Hotel, they sat near the window, from where they could see the main entrance of the hotel. The restaurant had very few people in it, which made Kanti slightly nervous. She would have preferred a crowded room so that their conversation would not be so intimate.

Prakash drew a deep breath and said, "You know, I agree with you. People shouldn't make hasty decisions about marriage. It's good you said that we should meet a few times more. Although"—here he smiled and played with his napkin—"I've already made up my mind."

"You shouldn't rush," Kanti said, worried that she sounded like a schoolteacher.

"You're right," he said. "You're absolutely right." He lowered his eyes. "It's just that I'm a little lonely."

"All the more reason not to," she said.

As they ate, some men wearing traditional Indian tapered trousers and long, flowing shirts set up musical instruments in a corner of the restaurant and started singing ghazals, their voices floating through the room, quieting conversations and the clatter of forks and knives. Once or twice when she glanced at Prakash, she found him engrossed in the music, with a sadness in his eyes that startled her.

The next morning she nearly bumped into Jaya turning a corner at Durbar Marg in front of the Royal Palace. He said, "Sorry" in a sulky tone.

She adjusted her shirt and, without thinking, said, "Can't you watch where you're going?"

He looked surprised, and they both burst out laughing. But he turned his back to her, leaned his arm against the building, and placed his forehead on it, convulsed with the hiccup-like laughter with which she was all too familiar.

She stood there, on the middle of the sidewalk, aware that people were looking at them with curiosity. She could not make up her mind whether to stay until Jaya faced her or whether to stop laughing and move on.

The next moment, Jaya turned around, his cheeks damp. He tried to frown and again broke into laughter.

"Come on, don't embarrass me," she said, bouncing her fist on his arm. The words and gesture broke whatever intimacy they'd just established, and he composed himself, a shadow on his face.

"How are you, Jaya?" she asked.

"Life continues," he said.

Standing there in front of Jaya, she suddenly did not care whom he had kissed and how many women he had slept with since they parted. And she wanted to say something more to him, to comfort him, comfort herself, make plans to meet, but she swallowed the words and phrases that came to her.

He looked at her expectantly, and when she didn't speak, he said, "I have to go. I have to meet someone."

She nodded, and he left.

At work that day Kanti was impatient with everyone and everything. "Are you ill, Kanti? Do you want to go home?" her supervisor asked, but she shook her head and pretended to be busy.

When everyone left the office in the evening, she picked up the phone and dialed Jaya's number. It came to her easily, ready on her fingertips. The phone rang for a long time. She wasn't surprised that Jaya was out, and his parents must have been on one of their trips abroad. She could imagine the servants out in the garden, the setting sun bathing the jasmine and marigolds in pink, the large stone Buddha in the middle, almost smiling, the servants laughing and joking, taking advantage of the free-dom, the phone by the stairs, the sound carrying to the corners of the big empty house.

She and Prakash went out again a few days later, this time to a rooftop restaurant in the center of the city, where they sat under a colorful garden umbrella. Prakash ordered beer, which surprised Kanti, because she hadn't seen him drink. Was he another Jaya? He said, with some embarrassment, "We should celebrate. You liked me enough to see me a second time." He persuaded her to order wine, which she barely touched all evening. She hoped he didn't think she was going to say yes just because she was with him again.

But he didn't broach the subject of marriage. They talked about his work, the problems he dealt with among his patients, his ambitions for the new clinic. She kept searching his face to see whether there were traces of the sadness she had seen last time. But this evening he was in a jovial mood, cracking jokes and asking her questions about America. Were Americans as wild as the Brits thought they were? Did she see Nelson Mandela in New York after his release? He kept ordering more beer, and she was worried that he might be drunk by the time dinner was over.

When they finished, it was already dark, and a light drizzle was falling. With a bit of a slur to his words, Prakash said, "I find rain romantic, don't you?"

"I don't know," she said. "Perhaps we should go."

They stood under an awning, waiting for a taxi. The rain began to splatter on the asphalt, and people ran to whatever shelter they could find. All the taxis that whizzed by were occupied. Prakash went upstairs to the restaurant to call for a taxi, and when he came down, she could see that his movements were still not coordinated.

The rain continued, and thunder rumbled overhead. Lightning streaked through the city, illuminating everything in sight. She caught a glimpse of Prakash's face and saw that his eyes were far away.

The cab he'd ordered appeared nearly twenty minutes later. When the driver asked where they were headed, Prakash, his hand casually on her arm, said, "Where are we going?"

"I want to go home," she said, surprised that he would think they would go anywhere else, in this rain, this late. She gave the driver her address.

After a few hundred yards, the cab stalled. The driver cursed, got out, and, instantly drenched with rain, opened the hood and tinkered with something. The car started but stopped again after a few yards. This happened three or four times, and the taxi finally refused to budge. Kanti asked the driver whether he could summon another taxi from the company, and the driver said, "How? I don't have a phone in here, and I don't see any shops around."

"We can walk," Prakash said. "It's not too far."

They stepped out of the taxi and were pelted with rain. Prakash linked his arm in hers, and she let him. They half-ran, half-walked to the house. Just as she reached to open the front door, Prakash said, "Kanti, may I tell you something before you go?"

"Here, in this rain? Why don't you come inside?"

"No, your mother is inside," he said. "Besides, we're already thoroughly soaked."

She waited.

"I know how you feel," he said.

"I don't understand."

"I mean, about that Rana boy."

It took a moment for Kanti to realize whom he was talking about; she never thought of Jaya as a Rana boy. "I don't want to talk about it," she said.

"I know how you feel," Prakash repeated. "I feel the same way. I understand you." His voice became strange, as if he were about to cry.

She saw a boy staring at them from a neighbor's house.

"I had a girlfriend," Prakash said. "In England." He paused. "I think of her all the time."

She didn't know what to say, so she remained quiet. A man walked by, holding a large umbrella.

"Her name was Sandy. She was from Kenya," he said. He touched her hand. "She was as beautiful as you are, Kanti. But she went to Kenya and never came back."

"Family obligations?" Her voice sounded cold to her.

"No, no," he said. "Her parents were dead. She had an elder

brother who was already married. She left me. She just decided that she didn't want me."

"Why wouldn't she want you?"

"Who knows? Maybe she didn't love me. Maybe she realized the difficulty—I mean, getting intimate with someone from a different culture. Maybe she's happily married now to a black man, has kids. I don't know why she left me." Prakash apparently realized that he sounded pathetic, for he straightened his shoulders and said, in a controlled voice, "I guess I wanted to tell you that I know the feeling."

"All relationships are not the same, Prakash-ji," she said, hoping he'd notice the distance the *ji* brought.

"I apologize," he said. "I didn't mean to probe."

"Good night." She opened the door, went inside, and closed it firmly behind her.

Inside, she leaned against the door and held still, water running down her legs and forming a pool around her feet. She looked toward her mother's room, and saw, through the narrow gap under the door, that the lights were off. Kanti knew that her mother was lying awake in bed, listening to the sound of the rain and the creaking of the door. Kanti slid down and sat on the floor. She wondered where Jaya was right now—probably in bed with some awful woman in a hotel. But, then, Kanti herself had been such a woman for a while.

Kanti got up and went to her room.

"Kanti, is that you?" her mother's voice rang faintly, but Kanti didn't respond.

The next morning Kanti gave her mother her decision about Prakash.

"But what happened? What's wrong with him?"

"Nothing is wrong with him," she said.

"Then?"

"I'm not ready, Mother."

"Not ready," her mother said, nodding slowly. "I understand. You want to be an old maid."

Her mother remained cold after this, replying to Kanti in monosyllables.

On the day she was to leave for North Carolina, Kanti tried calling Jaya. A servant told her that Jaya had left the country. No, the servant did not know where he had gone. "India perhaps? Maybe America?" He sounded as if the two countries were similar. Suddenly, fear gripped Kanti's belly. The fight in Gokarna, the two men . . . Jaya had gone looking for them, and now his body was lying . . . She shook her head.

At the airport Kanti smiled and talked to her relatives, telling them she would be back as soon as she finished her Ph.D. Her mother would not even look at her.

When the time came to go to her gate, Kanti faced her mother, who was now examining a poster advertising Thai Airlines.

"Talk with your daughter, Nirmala," one of the uncles said. "Who knows when you will see her again?"

"Mother, I will go now."

Her mother didn't turn.

"Mother."

Then she did turn, and Kanti saw that her eyes were filled with tears. Her mother took out a handkerchief, dabbed her eyes, and said, "All right."

As the plane lifted from the ground, with a thundering noise, Kanti noticed that the man across the aisle looked like Jaya—the black hair curling at the neck, the broad sulky forehead.

Clasping the arms of her seat as the plane tilted at a giddy angle, Kanti closed her eyes, and for a brief moment an image flitted across her mind: another man, perhaps darker than Jaya, someone at Duke or in New York or in another American city. The man had bright eyes and spoke gently. And then she saw herself, studying late at night in her room close to the university, or cupping snow in her palm and crunching it to feel its texture, or walking across the campus with new friends and professors, or looking into a mirror and seeing new shadows on her face.

Kanti opened her eyes and saw an elderly woman in the adjacent seat smiling at her. "Good, you're awake," the woman said. "Someone to talk to."

A Great Man's House

I STAYED because I could not bear the thought of abandoning a great man like my master. Last night, after she called me an "old pervert," I had thought about packing my meager belongings and finding another household where I could get a job as a cook. I tried to think of people in the city, mostly my master's friends, for whom I could work. When I realized that many wouldn't hire me because of my age, nearly sixty, I considered going back to my village near Dharan and opening a tea stall. I have fifteen thousand rupees locked inside the tin trunk in my room, the money I have saved during my eight years as a servant in this household. I thought about all these things, and in the end knew I could not leave my master to the mercy of his young wife, Nani Memsaheb. My master suffers from heart problems, severe back pains, and other ailments that keep him bedridden. Had I left, no one would have given my master his daily baths, cooked vegetarian food for him, washed his clothes, and cleaned his bed when he soiled it at night. Even as I make the evening dinner now, I hear him groaning in his room, the constant *ahhh* and *hummm* that have been his refrain for the past two years.

Earlier this afternoon, when I was boiling tea in the kitchen for Nani Memsaheb and her new lover, my master called my name. I went to his room, which is sparsely furnished, with one bed and with a straight-back chair where he used to sit and read before he became bedridden. He was lying on his back on the floor to ease the pain in his spine. The front of his shirt was soaked with sweat, and his eyelids were blue, sickly. Looking at him, I had to push away the memory that before Nani Memsaheb entered his life, he was a robust man, with shining eyes and a brisk walk.

"Ram Mohan, is my hot water bottle ready?" he asked me, his voice hoarse.

"Hajur, I was making tea for Nani Memsaheb. But I'll fix some hot water for you."

"Who is it this time?"

"He owns a hotel in Singapore," I told him. "I'll heat the water, hajur," and I quickly left the room. So far as I knew, the elderly man with Nani Memsaheb didn't own a hotel in Singapore. I had no idea of his occupation, but I mentioned the word "hotel" because my master and Nani Memsaheb own a well-known hotel in this city, and perhaps we could pretend that the man was here on business. In truth, this elderly man is a new member in her collection of lovers, most of whom don't last for a long time. But I also lied because I wanted to end the conversation. I did not want to know what my master was feeling at that moment.

I am still reeling from her insult yesterday. All I was trying to do was cover Nani Memsaheb with a blanket after she came home drunk and slumped on her bed without changing her sari. But as I was about to do so she opened her eyes and shouted at me.

Now, as I walked back to the kitchen from my master's

room, I heard laughter from the balcony upstairs. The men Nani Memsaheb brings to the house are invariably old, mostly my master's age, fifty or slightly younger. A few months ago there was one man in his late twenties, but he didn't last more than a week.

When I took the tea upstairs to the balcony, Nani Memsaheb was on a reclining chair, her eyes closed. The elderly man was singing to her. A long, slim cigarette burned in his fingers. I recognized the words from a Hindi song: "In this burning desire, I fall more deeply into a mire," and so on.

A smile was spread across her face, as if she were relishing every word coming out of his lips, and I wanted to laugh, because his voice was not that good.

When the man saw me standing behind him, he stopped singing, and a sour look came to his face. Her eyes still closed, Nani Memsaheb clasped his hand and said, "Don't stop, please."

He patted her hand and said, "Tea, Nani."

Then she saw me, and motioned with her finger that I was to put the tray down.

Nani Memsaheb has long, shining hair, and her eyes are dark and almost tearful, giving the impression that she is suffering, which, strangely, adds to her charm. She has delicate lips, which I imagine she frequently rubs with oil, because they are always glistening. When she smiles, it is as if she has granted you permission to be happy. Her only physical flaw is her slightly crooked nose; it leans to the left. But her face is so arresting that the nose seems only to be a sign of character.

She asked me to pour the tea. While I did, I tried to see whether she was still angry with me. But her face was calm, and she was focused on the man. He started his song again, stroking her chin as he sang. I finished pouring the tea and went downstairs.

My master was calling me again, so I hurried to the kitchen to heat water for him. As I turned on the gas, I was saddened, thinking of him in so much pain while his wife was entertaining another man in the house.

She was a different person when she used to visit my master before their marriage. It has been nearly five years since she first came to this house to see him, but I still remember the black sari she wore. She was twenty-five years old then. On that sultry day, I served omelettes to my master and Nani Memsaheb and her mother in the living room, and I somehow knew that a strong bond was already forming between my master and Nani Memsaheb, even though they'd met only moments before. Her mother, who was an acquaintance of my master, wore an ingratiating smile and was saying something to him, something about how much her daughter could learn from his spiritual guidance. My master kept nodding, but his eyes were glued to Nani Memsaheb, who only occasionally returned his look.

"I want you to come to our meetings," my master told Nani Memsaheb, even as her mother was talking to him. At that moment I was pouring tea for the mother, and I nearly spilled it on her lap. My master never invited young people to his weekly gatherings; he believed they had to experience the turbulence of life before they could turn their gaze inward. And for him to invite her right after they had met was even more unusual. I knew then that something strange was happening—and that it would turn out badly. But, of course, I say this after knowing everything that came to happen.

"I will happily come to your meetings," Nani Memsaheb said, in that small, demure voice she used during the early years.

On hearing her words, my master gave a slow, besotted smile.

At the time, my master had been a widower for nearly two years. His wife, whom I had never met, died in a motor car accident. A large framed picture of her still hangs in his room; she was a plain-looking woman with a broad face and horizontal strokes of sandalwood paste on her forehead, denoting her devotion to Shiva. She did not bear him any children. After her death, my master turned to religion, as if he were acknowledging his wife's heritage. He meditated regularly and practiced yoga. Sometimes when I entered his room, I found him performing the headstand, his legs stretched up toward the ceiling, one deformed big toe curved like a crescent moon. Initially I was amused that my master was trying so hard to look at the world upside down. Then I wondered how his head could carry the burden of his body, and why he didn't topple over. If I asked whether he wanted tea or anything to eat, he would not answer me. Later, he explained that he was doing Shirsasan, called the king of all poses because it reinvigorated the entire body. And he advised me not to speak to him when he did meditation or yoga, for that would interrupt the flow of energy. Of course, I did not completely understand what he was talking about, but I knew that the great saints of the past had devised these techniques to raise one's soul to a higher level.

Even I tried to perform Shirsasan a few times in my room. I did not tell my master I was doing so, but I placed my pillow on the floor, then leaned forward to rest my head on it, just as I had seen my master do. Slowly I attempted to lift my legs. But they wouldn't go up. Frustrated, I tried to jerk them up, but suddenly my back was on the floor, and the room was reeling. I gave up. Then I tried to meditate. I sat in the cross-legged position and tried to chant Om in my mind. But Om vanished as many other things demanded my attention: all the household details I had to take care of—washing my master's clothes, sweeping the veranda, going to the market to buy cauliflower and squash. Or, if I was in a melancholy or nostalgic mood, I would think of my village, of the gurgling stream that ran near the village square, of the surrounding small hills dotted with mud houses. Or I would question the details of my relatives' and neighbors' lives. Had Ghanshyam settled his land dispute with his brother? Had Kalidas married the woman he was lusting after? Had my old aunt, who was nearing ninety, lost all her vision yet? Often I would think of my wife, who had died of pneumonia years ago. After her death I had vowed I would never remarry. I am not sure why I made that vow, but at the time it seemed the proper thing to do. She was a loving, devoted woman, as religious as my master's dead wife, and I could not imagine trying to start life all over again with another woman. The images of my wife and questions about my relatives would become so insistent that eventually I sighed and gave up. I decided that meditation was for someone of a higher mind, like my master.

After he delved deeper into meditation and yoga, my master gained a reputation as a spiritual leader. Everyone spoke of him with reverence, even behind his back, which is rare in this city, where people search for others' character flaws. "Kailash-ji is a saint," some said. "A truly benevolent man." They pointed to his generosity, the temples he built, the money he donated to schools. Others praised him as an enlightened being, someone who understood the true nature of our universe and could help others reach a higher level of experience. They spoke of him as if he'd already achieved moksha, liberation from material cravings, even though he ran one of the most prosperous hotels in the city. People began to flock to him for advice, to hear him talk about the nature of the mind and the spirit. One admirer suggested that everyone would benefit if he delivered his talks on a regular basis, and thus was born the weekly spiritual ses-

sion. It was indeed surprising that my master acquired, quickly
and effortlessly, the reputation of a spiritual leader, given that
he had barely started his journey on the spiritual path in a country teeming with gurus and religious leaders, who often earned
their status only after years of study and reflection. But my
master had something in him that the others didn't have, a nat-
ural energy that made troubled souls want to talk to him, tell
him their life stories, an aura that made people feel that their
merely being in his presence would attain peace for their minds.

Before Nani Memsaheb started visiting regularly, my master
and I spent long periods of time alone, except for the weekends,
when his relatives visited, and the evenings when the guests
came for the spiritual sessions. On weekdays, he would come
back late from the hotel, not the least bit tired after a full day's
work. I would cook for him—beans and peas and spinach—
while he immersed himself in his yoga and meditation, and
then we would eat. Some evenings I would massage his feet
by the bed when he wasn't reading from his collection of great
religious and philosophical texts—the Bhagavad Gita, the Pa-
tanjali Yoga Pradipa, the Ramayana, the Upanishads, and Buddhist sutras. I remember these, because whenever I dusted my
master's bookshelves, I would finger the spines of these books
and wonder whether I'd ever be able to understand their mar-
velous secrets. On the other hand, I was always glad when my
master chose not to read in the evenings. Never did I feel as
satisfied and peaceful as when I massaged my master's feet in
the quiet of the evening and watched his face as he fell asleep.
Then I forgot my own concerns: the bones that seemed to be
rotting inside me from age, the distance I had drifted from
my village, the thoughts of my dead wife. I felt I was once again
a child.

We were not alone in the house all the time. Every Saturday

afternoon, many of my master's relatives came, and brought along their servants to help me cook. Although I never liked so many servants running around my kitchen and misplacing my things, I did not complain, because my master seemed to enjoy the noise and the conversation. One of the servants was Laxmi, a seventeen-year-old Tamang girl who worked in my master's uncle's house. I could not help noticing that Laxmi had an open face and a lithe body. She was a bit of a tease, and I used to enjoy it when our bodies brushed against each other in that crowded kitchen, even though I knew I was too old to be thinking about her that way. "This Ram Mohan dai," Laxmi used to say, loudly, so that everyone could hear, "his teeth are falling out, and his hands are everywhere."

At first the servants laughed, but after a few weeks I noticed a strained look on her face every time I came near her. She no longer teased me, and the other servants no longer laughed when I cracked a joke about her. One day after they left, before the evening guests arrived, my master came into the kitchen and said, "Ram Mohan, why don't you go back to your village for a few days? See your relatives. Maybe even get married again. Now that you have some money, I'm sure you'll be able to find a suitable bride." When I said that I didn't want to, he said, "Our physical needs are important. We can't deny them, no matter how old we get." I washed again some dishes the other servants had left with food particles clotted on the surface. "Think about it," my master said. "You can bring her here, and she can live with us." He was chewing an apple. "One always needs to be aware of what one's body wants. Our body is our soul."

I knew what my master was saying. When Laxmi's body touched mine, I had become aroused, and this was wrong, especially for an old man like me. Often in bed at night, I worried that my impulses sometimes got the better of me, but just thinking about my impulses aroused me even more. I had never felt this way when my wife was alive or before I came to work in my master's house, and was perplexed that my desires grew as I got older. What could I now say to my master? So I said, "Shall I make you some tea, hajur?"

My master shook his head and left. His words did open up a possibility I had not allowed myself to consider, but I knew that going back to the village and searching for a wife would be too great an effort. It didn't, however, prevent me from imagining what a new wife might look like (if, indeed, I were to marry, which I knew I would not), but every time I tried to visualize her, I saw the face of Nani Memsaheb, who had, at this time, visited the house only a couple of times. I found this disturbing, so much so that once, while I was standing in the kitchen, a saucer slipped out of my hand and shattered on the floor.

On Saturday afternoons, when the relatives left at around four, I would set up comfortable chairs on the big balcony upstairs and a wooden platform with cushions for my master to sit on. I would clean the house and prepare it for the arrival of the evening guests. The guests were invariably men, often as old as my master. Once in a while I'd spot an elderly woman in the group, but no woman ever came on a regular basis.

Nani Memsaheb started coming by herself to these evening talks. She would sit quietly in a corner, with that shy look on her face, while my master spoke. I served the guests tea and remained as much in the background as possible. Every now and then, a guest would politely ask a question or make a comment, but mostly my master talked, his voice clear, soothing in the evening air. The first evening she came, all the men looked puzzled, and some raised their eyebrows. But my master offered no explanation; he didn't even introduce her to the rest of the group. He continued his talk as if nothing unusual had happened, as if the beautiful woman who just sat down, dressed in a black sari, with long, heavy silver earrings glinting through her hair, her face glowing like a full moon, was not a distraction. I wondered whether she wore black clothes to hold my master's attention.

Those who attended these sessions were men whose minds surely constantly dwelled on deep philosophical subjects; they listened attentively as my master spoke, interrupting only to ask questions. I watched Nani Memsaheb as she gazed at my master's face. When their eyes met occasionally, she quickly looked down, crimson spreading across her cheeks. Once, her eyes filled with tears, and I remember thinking—the thought came from nowhere and disappeared instantly—she is going to be the death of him. My master often talked about the impermanence of thought, and how meditation could make us aware of this. That's what happened to me: my thought came and vanished. But, as I remember to this day what I thought then, perhaps thoughts are not fragile and fleeting after all. Perhaps they are solid, rooting themselves in our brain even while giving the impression that they are no longer there.

Soon, Nani Memsaheb became a regular part of the household. She helped me cook food and prepare for the Saturday afternoon gatherings, which annoyed my master's relatives, because they saw that as a sign of her increasing authority in the house. "Ram Mohan dai," Laxmi said in the kitchen one day while Nani Memsaheb was using the phone, "this house is not the same as it used to be."

The other servants nodded.

"I don't want to come here anymore," Laxmi said.

One of my master's cousins, an enormous woman with a swinging walk, came into the kitchen and said, "What's happening in this house, huh, Ram Mohan? What's going on?"—as if I'd invited Nani Memsaheb to join us each weekend. "Just because someone new comes in, does that mean we are to be ignored?" She said this loudly, and everyone knew that she meant my master and Nani Memsaheb to hear. My master hadn't exactly been ignoring his relatives, but in Nani Memsaheb's presence he often seemed to forget that others were around. I shrugged my shoulders and kept washing the dishes. In a few minutes Nani Memsaheb came in and asked me to peel the fruit for the evening guests. Everyone was quiet. "Did you hear, Ram Mohan?" Nani Memsaheb asked, and I wiped my hands on a towel and took the fruit from the refrigerator. My master's cousin fingered Nani Memsaheb's earrings and said, "Where did you buy these? I want to get some for myself."

Day by day, I watched Nani Memsaheb move around the house as if she had lived here a long time. She spent time in the kitchen, helping me or giving me instructions. She sat on the living room floor and, with her small, square glasses perched on her nose, read from my master's collection of books. In the hallway, she rearranged and replaced the black-and-white photographs of temples. One night, she did not go home after spending the day. She went into my master's bedroom, bolted the door, and stayed all night. That night I did not go to the small outhouse in the garden assigned to me but used my master's bathroom. Although I listened intently, I couldn't hear any noise coming from his bedroom. Soon I was ashamed and hurried back to my room.

From then on, my master and Nani Memsaheb were inseparable. Whenever he looked at her, he seemed to forget who was where and what was what. She began to call him "my old man," but in a sweet voice. She even accompanied him to the hotel, and soon she was named the general manager, much to the dismay of many relatives, who had been after my master for years to get them jobs there. Since I never went to the hotel, I don't know what the staff thought of her, but I heard from the relatives, who now came to me regularly to complain about her, that she was not popular, that the hotel was falling apart because of her bad management. I knew, of course, that there could be no truth to these accusations. First, my master would never have allowed such a thing to happen, and second, she had made several improvements in the house. She'd had the walls painted white, hired two gardeners to make the garden bloom with flowers and leaves, extended the kitchen so that I would have more space to work, and built a balcony upstairs that afforded a tremendous view of the Pashupatinath Temple and the Shivapuri Mountain. After a while, I became accustomed to her authority, and went to her instead of to my master if I had a question. Sometimes I resented how quickly she had established power in such a great man's house, but most often I admired the way she'd done it.

"I know what she wants," my master's cousin whispered to me one Saturday afternoon. "She will eventually have the hotel and this house put under her own name, throw him, and you, out of her life, and then marry a young stud." She leaned closer to me so that I got a whiff of her stale-radish breath, that mouth into which she stuffed food all day. "This old man–young woman thing never works. And she, she has all kinds of plans for herself."

I kept quiet, for I didn't feel comfortable talking about Nani Memsaheb with jealous relatives. But I did recall the premonition I had had when Nani Memsaheb first visited the house, and later that night I wondered whether she had attached herself to my master for money.

On the evening of their marriage, red, green, and yellow lights blinking on the roof made the house look joyous. A large tent was set up on the lawn, under which a buffet of twenty-two dishes was laid out. An army band played popular songs in a corner, and some children danced, drawing laughter from everyone. Relatives of my master, many from the village where he was born, came to celebrate. The relatives who knew Nani Memsaheb sighed and looked at one another as if to say, "What can we do?" But in the presence of the couple, they too acted happy. "You are a lucky man, hajur," his cousin told him, gobbling a large piece of cake. "Such a beautiful wife, one who loves you so much." The rest of the relatives nodded, their faces beaming.

During the wedding ceremony, I got such painful stomach cramps that I had to leave the lawn many times. Nani Memsaheb's mother teased me about gorging myself on the food, but I told her I hadn't eaten much, that it was something else.

After everyone left, I watched my master and Nani Memsaheb retreat to their bedroom. Sitting on the veranda, I listened to the noises of the night, the frogs, the occasional blare of a horn in the distance, people shouting one another's names. I tried to concentrate on these noises and block out the muffled voices coming from my master's bedroom. My stomach cramps had subsided, and I could more easily focus on the sounds of the neighborhood. I tried not to think about anything else, and before long I realized that I was actually attempting to meditate. For the first time, meditation came to me, perhaps because of the tremendous sadness in me, sadness for myself for having reached an old age with nothing to show but my service to my master, who now was in the arms of a woman half his age, a woman who would, I was convinced, bring pain and suffering to the house.

After the marriage, Nani Memsaheb started calling me Ramey, a nickname I disliked. It did not have the dignity of Ram Mohan. My master smiled when he saw me wince at the nickname. "It's her affectionate name for you, Ram Mohan," he said. "She has made you her own with that name."

That night, in my room, my mind kept repeating the words "made you her own." I whispered them aloud, and, oddly, began to like the sound of them. Before long, I realized that I was getting aroused. An incredible feeling of shame washed over me, and I quickly got up from my bed and went outside. The Ghantaghar clock tower in the city's center announced midnight. A full moon was shining. I reached my arms behind my back and strolled through the garden, trying to calm myself. I was troubled by this excitement and the shame that accompanied it.

I heard the balcony door creak open, and I looked up to see Nani Memsaheb, wearing only a petticoat and a bra, leaning against the railing and gazing up at the moon. Her long hair ran down her shoulders and her back. I couldn't help staring. When she took her eyes from the moon and saw me there in the garden, she froze for a moment, then quickly went inside.

The next morning when I brought tea to their bedroom at the usual time, Nani Memsaheb and my master were still asleep, her arm on his chest and her thigh beneath her petticoat over his legs. I set the tea by the bedside, my legs shaking slightly, my eyes riveted on Nani Memsaheb's thigh. My master opened his eyes and said, "Isn't it early for tea, Ram Mohan?"

"It's already eight o'clock, hajur," I said.

My master patted her thigh and said, "Nani, tea."

She yawned and said, "Was that you last night in the garden, Ramey?"

I shook my head, trying to show surprise.

"It wasn't you?" She was watching my face closely.

"I was in bed all night."

"I could have sworn it was you," she said. "Or someone who looked like you."

"You have a twin brother, Ram Mohan?" my master said and laughed.

I forced a smile and left the room.

A few weeks after the wedding, my master's weekly meetings resumed, and Nani Memsaheb joined the older men, as she had done before. As usual, my master spoke at length, and the others interrupted only to ask for clarifications or make brief observations. During one session, about two months after the wedding, while I was serving tea to the guests, Nani Memsaheb interrupted my master while he was speaking. My master had been talking about the nature of the mind, how it moves from one place to another like a monkey, and how in order to reach a higher level, one has to control that monkey. Put it on a leash, my master had said, so that it cannot run around. Then the mind will become one with the Brahman.

"But when once we have the monkey on a leash," she said, smiling faintly, "then we too are tethered to the leash, aren't we?"

My master smiled, affectionately, understandingly, as one smiles at a child. "Yes, we are. The trick is to be tethered to that leash while also controlling it."

"But how is that possible?" she asked. "It seems to me that the trick is not to have the monkey on a leash at all. Let the monkey do whatever it wants. Why become attached to it?"

An old gentlemen with a mustache, a high government official, said, "Let's listen to him fully before we offer comments."

My master was still smiling, and he didn't speak for a short while, until the old gentleman said, "Please go on."

Throughout the rest of the session, Nani Memsaheb said nothing. A deep crease had appeared on her forehead. My master glanced at her a few times while he spoke, but she didn't look back at him; her eyes roamed the faces of the men who were listening to her husband.

After they left, the two sat down to dinner as if no disagreement had occurred. She kept offering him more food, and he kept thanking her graciously.

From then on, Nani Memsaheb continually interrupted my master during the sessions. Once she even muttered, "Rubbish," in a voice loud enough for everyone to hear. My master lost track of what he was saying, and his eyes turned cloudy. The other men frowned at her, and one guest coughed. Another time she let out a giggle, which she tried to a disguise as a hiccup. My master paused, a concerned look on his face, and said, "Why don't you drink some water, Nani?"

I was disturbed by the way she challenged his authority, the vast knowledge he had acquired through years of reading and contemplating. I despised the strident manner in which she offered her opinions, and the crease, now permanent, on her forehead. But late at night, when I lay in bed, when my mind quieted and I could hear my own breathing, it seemed to me absurd that in a group of learned men, it was a much younger woman who didn't buy the high-minded thoughts of my master's. Even stranger, once the guests left, Nani Memsaheb and my master would joke and laugh, talk about the hotel, as if nothing had happened. They never discussed spiritual matters, as if some unwritten rule forbade them from such debates outside those sessions. Now I think that, had they talked about their disagreements in the privacy of their bedroom, some of the resentment and the tension would have cleared.

Not long after, Nani Memsaheb started questioning my

master's judgment about matters in the house and the hotel. We were in the kitchen, and they were discussing the poor performance of the hotel's restaurant manager, a woman my master had hired a few years before. My master was saying that he wanted to transfer her to the laundry room, because she had developed a hostile attitude toward the restaurant staff, in particular the assistant manager, who was known for his hard work and efficiency.

"That's ridiculous," Nani Memsaheb said abruptly.

My master didn't say anything for a while. With a vague smile on his face, he said softly, "Nani, the staff have been complaining to me for months now. Something must be done."

"She's fine the way she is," she said. "Where she is."

"Why do you say that?"

"Because." Nani Memsaheb sipped her tea and looked out the window. "You think I don't know what goes on in there? They don't like her because she's a woman and she tells them what to do."

"It's not like that at all, Nani. She's having a bad effect on their morale. She screams at them, insults them. The assistant manager told me that she even threw water on him the other day for some small mistake he had made."

She replied, "She threw water on him because he laughed when she asked him to rearrange the south room tables."

"Still," my master said cautiously, as if something were stuck in his throat, "the chef told me that she dumped his perfectly fine chicken chili in the garbage."

"She dumped it in the garbage because it tasted like garbage." She pointed at me. "Even our Ramey here cooks better than that chef."

I tried not to appear insulted.

My master looked at me, then down at his fingers.

That night I prayed to Lord Ganesh, whose small framed picture hangs on my wall, that he make everything better in the house, the way it was before. But even as I prayed, my eyes closed, my palms joined in supplication, I knew that would not happen. In fact, at that point I had a vision. With my eyes closed, I saw a young man with Nani Memsaheb, and she was laughing with him. At first the man was a stranger. Then slowly his face became mine — me, with a smooth, youthful face — and I quickly opened my eyes, my heart pounding, and stared at the picture of Lord Ganesh, with his long snout and his doe-like eyes, which at that moment were mocking me.

One Saturday during the winter month of Meen Pachas, a time so cold that even the fish are said to be frozen, I was taking my early morning bath by the water pump in the garden. I find the cold water and the smell of the earth just as light breaks in the sky invigorating. Normally I have this time to myself, so I was surprised and slightly irritated at Nani Memsaheb's appearance. She couldn't see me, because the pump is hidden behind bushes. I quietly turned off the water. Through an opening, I saw that she was crying, her arms tightly hugging her chest. Occasionally she looked up at the sky, as if searching for an answer in the heavens. I kept watching her, mesmerized. She paced in the garden for a while, then wiped her face and went inside.

For a long time, I stood by the pump, shivering, but ignoring the cold, wearing only my dhoti, which clung to my skin.

Some of the older men stopped coming to the evening sessions. One said to me, at the end of his last session, "Ram Mohan, this house is not the same anymore."

He had come to the kitchen to get a glass of water, although there was always a carafe full of water on the balcony. He took some pills from his pocket and swallowed them, leaned against the counter, and sighed. "Amazing what a woman can do."

I didn't voice my opinion.

"Well, this is it. I have decided." And he walked down the stairs and out of the house.

One by one, the others stopped coming. Soon, there were only four who attended, then two.

One evening a big argument erupted between Nani Memsaheb and the high government official with the mustache. As usual, she had interrupted my master. "No, I don't think you are anywhere close to the truth. It's very easy for you to sit up there on that cushion and preach on the illusions that our desires create. But the truth is this, that most ordinary people like me want to learn how to live and fulfill our desires, not treat them as if they were stepchildren. For us—"

"Quiet!" the mustached man shouted.

There was silence.

Nani Memsaheb looked at him contemptuously and said, "And why should I be quiet?"

His voice quivered. "Because you don't know anything."

"And you do?"

"Nani," my master warned.

"I know a lot more than you do," the man said.

"I have yet to see evidence of that."

The other man, small, with a bulbous nose, said to Nani Memsahib, "What is this? Aren't you ashamed to be doing this?"

"Leave it be," my master said.

"She's a woman," the small man said, "and she doesn't know her place." To my master, he said, "Sorry, Kailash-ji, I didn't want to say anything. But this has become unbearable."

"Get out," Nani Memsaheb said.

Both men watched her, and my master said, "Peace, everyone. It's a small thing."

"Get out of my house," Nani Memsaheb told the two men. She stood. "Now. Quickly. You come to my house and you want to put me in my place. Go home, and do that to your mothers and wives." Before anyone knew what she was doing, she picked up one of my slippers near the door and started to beat the two men.

"Nani!" my master shouted. It was the first time he had raised his voice in a long time.

But Nani Memsaheb kept hitting the two men with my slipper (my slipper!), and they hastily stood and put on their shoes. She backed away and watched them, a thick strand of hair falling down her forehead, her face flushed. My master moved toward the men and tried to pat their arms, but they brushed his hand away. "We didn't come here to be insulted like this," they said. "Kailash-ji, you'd better control your woman. Otherwise she will destroy you."

They left, muttering, their faces red.

My master hit her. He slapped her so hard that she fell back a couple of steps.

She put her hand to her cheek and said, "All right."

He immediately apologized, but Nani Memsaheb kept repeating, "All right," and she went to their bedroom. We heard the door being locked.

My master sat down weakly. I poured him a glass of water, which he seemed to swallow in one gulp. He started to sob. I didn't know what to do.

I went to the kitchen and finished the dishes. As I was about to go to my room, I heard murmurs coming from their room. I stood next to their door and, judging from the words "my old man" and "Nanu," it was obvious that they had made up.

★

A few days later they had another argument, and my master had a heart attack. They were sitting at the dining room table, waiting for me to serve dinner. I don't recall what Nani Memsaheb said, but my master responded, in a sharp, hurt tone, "Of course, my thoughts don't matter, my feelings don't matter." His face flushed, then turned gray, and he started to rub his chest and groan. I was holding a bowl of chickpeas, so I could only watch as his chair tipped and he fell to the floor. Nani Memsaheb rushed to him, shouting his name.

"We must take him to the hospital," I said, and ran to the neighbor's house to look for Krishna, who could drive, because my master's regular driver had already gone home.

In the car, Nani Memsaheb cradled my master's head in her lap. His eyes were closed. "Don't leave me," she said, and repeated the words, rocking her head above his ashen face till we reached the hospital.

It turned out that my master had had a minor heart attack, and after he spent a couple of days in the hospital, the doctors let him leave, with detailed instructions to Nani Memsaheb about his care. For a few days, she didn't leave his side.

"I'll resume yoga again, soon," he told her. "Not to worry." He had lost a great deal of weight; his cheeks were caved in, and his eyes were dim and hesitant.

"No yoga until you get better."

"But yoga helps—"

"No arguments," she said. It was obvious from her appearance that she had done her share of crying in the past days.

He smiled feebly and repeated, "No arguments."

Although they did not argue for a few weeks, my master's body was going through an argument of its own. His fifty-second birthday was approaching, but he looked sixty, with new lines on his face and his breathing erratic and raspy. Twice he had to be taken to the hospital because he had difficulty breathing. Each time he came back, he looked worse.

"The doctor told me to keep him relaxed," Nani Memsaheb said, and as she noticed that I was looking at her strangely, she added, her expression slightly guilty, "We'll have to be careful not to upset him." I have done nothing, I thought.

During those weeks, Nani Memsaheb stayed with him in their bedroom. He even had difficulty walking to the bathroom, but that didn't stop him from worrying that the hotel would fall apart without their supervision.

"The hotel can go to hell," Nani Memsaheb said. "Your health is more important."

When some of my master's friends came to see him, they didn't speak to Nani Memsaheb. The mustached gentleman curtly nodded at her and smiled at my master. "Kailash-ji, we like to see you healthy and happy," he said, and my master responded that he was healthy and happy, that this was just a cosmic test to challenge his resolve. They exchanged a few spiritual jokes about swamis.

The small man with the big nose came the next day and would not look at Nani Memsaheb as she ushered him to my master's bedside. The man spoke at length about some Ayurvedic treatment for the heart, which had cured one of his friends.

But over time my master's health did not improve, and Nani Memsaheb became absent-minded, often forgetting and losing things. Once she went to the market and came back empty-handed. "I forgot," she said. "I tried, but I couldn't remember what I went for."

I gave her a glass of water.

"It was as if my thoughts had become breathless, Ramey, as if someone were choking them." She was ready to cry, I could tell, but she left before she did so in my presence.

When she cooked for my master, which she now sometimes insisted on doing, she would forget to turn off the gas in the stove, and in about an hour, the entire house smelled of rotten eggs. In the afternoons she retreated to the living room, and when I took tea to her, I would find her on the sofa, holding her head as if someone had hit her. "Tea, Nani," I said, and she would look up with dull, dry eyes.

Finally, Nani Memsaheb asked her mother to come live with us, an idea I didn't like, because I partly blamed her mother for bringing Nani Memsaheb into this house. But it was clear that taking care of my master had exhausted Nani Memsaheb, so I reconciled myself to the idea of her mother's moving in.

Nani Memsaheb's mother turned out to be an excellent nurse to my master, who now was being taken to a doctor every week. She also proved to be an agreeable person, and I didn't mind her help in the kitchen. After she came to live with us, Nani Memsaheb began to spend less time with my master. She'd stay at the hotel all day, sometimes until late at night. I couldn't believe the hotel needed such constant supervision, but she finally gained back some of her color and started to smile more often. It was also clear that she looked forward to getting out of the house every morning.

What startled me was how my master had been transformed from a healthy, robust person to a coughing, wheezing, sputtering old man. All those years of yoga and meditation and all that high-minded talk. I conceded that maybe Nani Memsaheb was right. Maybe we shouldn't worry about tethering the monkey to the leash; maybe we should forget about the monkey and, instead of constantly trying to achieve higher levels of existence, live our lives like ordinary human beings. But when I tried to imagine what the situation might have been had Nani

Memsaheb not entered the picture, I could see my master still surrounded by his adoring relatives, conducting the spiritual sessions, and me massaging his feet each night. I felt nostalgic and couldn't help being critical of Nani Memsaheb.

My master appeared relieved that it was his wife's mother, and not his wife, who tended to his needs day and night. Only occasionally did he reveal any anguish. One night he simply refused to drink the soup Nani Memsaheb's mother was trying to feed him with a spoon. "Come, Kailash-ji," she coaxed. "It'll help you sleep properly."

But he crossed his arms and pressed his lips together like a child.

"What's the matter?" she said.

I was standing in the doorway, watching with sadness.

My master looked at me and said, "Where is she?"

"She's at the hotel, hajur."

"This late?" He winced in pain, shook his head.

Nani Memsaheb's mother held the spoon close to his mouth. "Eat," she said.

"I want Nani to feed me," he said.

"But she's not here."

"I don't care," he said. "I want her."

We had to plead with him for nearly half an hour before he finally drank the soup.

Rumors started circulating that Nani Memsaheb was spending time with men in the hotel and around the city, mostly older, well-off men like my master. His cousin came to visit one day and whispered to me in the kitchen, "She's behaving like a prostitute, Ram Mohan. He should never have married her."

I put her ridiculous talk out of my mind until the evening Nani Memsaheb brought home a gray-haired man in a suit. I heard her tell her mother that he was a casino manager at the largest hotel in the city, and that he was offering advice on how to start a casino in my master's hotel. Her mother was quiet throughout dinner as Nani Memsaheb and the man laughed with a disturbing familiarity. She didn't even introduce him to my master, and after the man left, she and her mother argued behind closed doors in the living room. Their voices were loud, so I heard everything, and I shut the door to my master's room. Her mother demanded to know about her relationship with that man, and Nani Memsaheb retorted that she didn't need to answer to anyone in this world, and that if it wasn't for her, her mother would be out in the streets, begging. I believed that my master, even though he was asleep in his room, had an idea of what was going on.

In the following months, Nani Memsaheb brought all sorts of men to the house. They were much older than she, almost my master's age. There was the chief accountant of a travel agency, a thin man who said almost nothing. The next man was a kuirey journalist, a white foreigner with body odor, who spoke to Nani Memsaheb in English. There was a businessman, the owner of a fan-manufacturing company. There were others; I don't remember all of them.

What I do remember is the big fight Nani Memsaheb had with her mother that took place the night the kuirey journalist came for dinner. As soon as Nani Memsaheb closed the door behind him, still smiling at something he had said, her mother grabbed her hand and led her into the living room, where, once again behind closed doors, they argued. This time, I heard them throw things at each other. Her mother called her a whore, and Nani Memsaheb retorted that her mother was the one who had made her that way.

"What's the matter?" my master called out in his weak voice.

When they opened the door and came out, Nani Memsaheb's mother was crying. The next morning, she packed her
clothes and left in a taxi. Nani Memsaheb didn't even say goodbye to her.

For a few days Nani Memsaheb stayed home, tending to my
master. She took care of him with a diligence that made me
optimistic. I thought that perhaps she wasn't such a terrible
person after all, and that the argument with her mother had
made her realize the error of her ways. But soon she grew restless, and reverted to the routine of staying out late. She also
started to drink. I was surprised when she came home one
night, swaying on her feet. I asked whether she was all right,
and she said, her tongue thick, "Of course I'm all right, Ramey.
Why wouldn't I be?" And she tripped on the staircase.

My master is in constant pain these days, and all that is left of
him are gray skin and thinning bones. He can hardly get out of
bed, and beside him on the night table are enough tablets, cap-
sules, and syrups to make a healthy man ill. When he has to
take care of his needs, he calls me, and I bring him a basin,
which I then empty in the bathroom. Even though the stench is
often overwhelming, I look at his face, the way pain has made
his eyes pale and dull, and I don't mind. He was a great man
once, and he's still a great man as far as I am concerned. As he
used to say, the body is only a vehicle for the soul, and the soul
has no physical form.

Right now as I stand in the kitchen waiting for my master or
Nani Memsaheb to call me, all I can think of is how she shouted
at me last night, and I am covered with anger and shame.

She came home late from the hotel, smelling of alcohol. I
was about to serve her dinner when she drunkenly waved her

hand and said, "No food, Ramey, no food." She lingered at the door of my master's room, her forehead resting against the wood frame, and after a while she staggered upstairs to her room.

I finished the dishes, turned off all the lights, and stood in the darkness, listening to the sounds of the night. Then I walked upstairs to make sure that her lights were off and her windows closed. The house was very quiet, and as I headed down the hallway, the only sound was of a dog barking in the distance. Her door was ajar, and light filtered into the hall. I pushed open the door softly and walked inside. She was lying in bed in the black sari with red-flower patterns she'd worn that evening. Her breathing was heavy, and the end of the sari had slid down, exposing her navel and the rise and fall of her breasts. Even in sleep, the deep crease cut across her forehead, and her left eyelid was fluttering. I watched her for some time. Then I closed the windows and picked up the blanket folded at the end of her bed. I was about to drape it over her when a tightness in my throat and chest made my legs tremble. As I lowered the blanket over her breasts, she abruptly opened her eyes and said, "Ramey." Her eyes moved to my hand, and she shouted, "You old pervert!" I swallowed and left the room.

Why was I overcome with that strange feeling? Why, at this age, did my legs shake at the sight of her navel? Since last night I have tried to calm my frantic thoughts by chanting Om, but my thoughts have a life of their own and refuse to obey me.

My master probably won't live more than a few months. What will Nani Memsaheb do then? Will she wear a widow's white dhoti, leave off her makeup, and devote her thoughts to her departed husband? Highly unlikely. What will happen to me? Will she continue to use my services? Or will she let me go?

Thinking that far ahead worries me. I must keep my thoughts focused on the present: the cauliflower frying in the hot oil; the sound of our neighbors, a gambler husband and a rancorous wife, arguing; a child playing outside in the dark, mumbling about ghosts and demons; my hands, through years of washing and cooking, now veined, old, tired.

Made in the USA
San Bernardino, CA
14 March 2014